Ninja Air Fryer
Recipe Book UK

Simplify Your Cooking with Easy-to-Follow Ninja Foodi Air Fryer Recipes That Deliver Unbeatable Taste and Texture | Colours to Inspire Your Culinary Creativity

Drucilla Vaughn

© Copyright 2024 –All Rights Reserved

This document is geared towards providing exact and reliable information concerning the topic and issue covered.

In no way is it legal to reproduce, duplicate, or transmit any part of this document in either electronic means or printed format. Recording this publication is strictly prohibited. Any storage of this document is not allowed unless with written permission from the publisher.

All rights reserved. The information provided herein is stated to be truthful and consistent, in that any liability, in terms of inattention or otherwise, by any usage or abuse of any policies, processes, or directions contained within is the solitary and utter responsibility of the recipient reader.

Under no circumstances will any legal responsibility or blame be held against the publisher for any reparation, damages, or monetary loss due to the information herein, either directly or indirectly. Respective authors own all copyrights not held by the publisher.

The information herein is offered for informational purposes solely and is universal as so. The presentation of the information is without a contract or any type of guarantee assurance. The trademarks used are without any consent, and the publication of any trademark is without permission or backing by the trademark owner.

All trademarks and brands within this book are for clarifying purposes only, are owned by the owners themselves, and are not affiliated with this document.

Contents

Introduction	01
Fundamentals of Ninja Air Fryer Max	02
4-Week Meal Plan	10
Chapter 1 Breakfast	12
Chapter 2 Vegetables and Sides	20
Chapter 3 Snacks and Starters	27
Chapter 4 Poultry	34
Chapter 5 Fish and Seafood	43
Chapter 6 Beef and Pork	52
Chapter 7 Desserts	61
Chapter 6 Beef and Pork	61
Conclusion	69
Appendix Recipes Index	70

Introduction

The Ninja Air Fryer Recipe Book UK is the ultimate guide to mastering the art of air frying. With vibrant, full-colour images accompanying every recipe, this cookbook is designed to inspire both beginners and seasoned chefs alike. The Ninja Air Fryer has revolutionised home cooking, allowing you to prepare crispy, healthy meals with little to no oil. Whether you're cooking for a busy family or hosting a gathering, this book offers a wide variety of recipes that cater to every taste and occasion.

From savoury breakfasts to indulgent desserts, each recipe is carefully crafted to bring out the best in your air fryer. The step-by-step instructions make cooking easy, while the helpful tips ensure perfect results every time. You'll find a range of recipes, from quick and simple snacks to more elaborate meals, all designed to fit into your busy lifestyle without sacrificing flavour.

The cookbook is not just about air frying; it's a celebration of healthy, delicious eating. With a focus on fresh ingredients and minimal fuss, it helps you make the most of your Ninja Air Fryer Max's versatility. Whether you're in the mood for crispy fries, succulent meats, or baked goods, this book will guide you through it all, making it your go-to companion in the kitchen.

Fundamentals of Ninja Air Fryer Max

The Ninja Air Fryer Max is a versatile kitchen appliance designed to cook food quickly and efficiently using hot air circulation. With a powerful 1750-watt heating element, it provides a rapid, even cook, creating crispy and golden results with little to no oil. With it, you don't have to worry about not being able to cook well. Next we learn the basic information about Ninja Air Fryer Max.

What is the Ninja Air Fryer Max?

The Ninja Air Fryer Max is a powerful kitchen appliance designed to bring convenience, speed, and versatility to your cooking experience. This innovative air fryer allows you to prepare crispy, delicious meals with little to no oil, using the magic of hot air circulation. With a large capacity and advanced technology, the Ninja Air Fryer Max is perfect for families or anyone who enjoys preparing a variety of dishes with ease.

The key feature of the Ninja Air Fryer Max is its Max Crisp Technology, which enables it to reach a higher temperature of up to 240°C (475°F), giving you the ability to cook food faster than traditional methods while ensuring it's crispy on the outside and tender on the inside. Whether you're cooking fresh ingredients, frozen foods, or even baking, this air fryer makes it all possible.

Equipped with a 5.2-litre (5.5-quart) basket, the Ninja Air Fryer Max provides ample space to cook enough food for the whole family or a small gathering. It's not just limited to frying, though; it offers multiple cooking functions including air frying, roasting, baking, reheating, and dehydrating, making it a versatile tool for all your cooking needs. The wide temperature ranges from 40°C to 240°C (105°F to 475°F) also ensures that it can handle a variety of recipes, from crispy chicken wings to homemade crisps, vegetables, and even cakes.

The Ninja Air Fryer Max is incredibly user-friendly, featuring a digital touchscreen with easy-to-understand buttons and preset cooking programmes for quick meals. The non-stick basket and crisper plate make cleaning a breeze, while the compact design allows for easy storage.

In short, the Ninja Air Fryer Max combines powerful functionality with ease of use, making it an essential addition to any kitchen. Whether you're a busy professional or a home cook, this appliance helps you create healthier, tastier meals in a fraction of the time.

How Does Ninja Air Fryer Max Work?

The Ninja Air Fryer Max operates through a combination of advanced technologies and user-friendly features to deliver efficient and healthier cooking. Here's how it works:

Max Crisp Technology: This feature allows the air fryer to reach temperatures up to 240°C (475°F), enabling faster cooking times and achieving a crispier texture on foods.

Rapid Air Circulation: A powerful fan circulates hot air around the food, ensuring even cooking and browning without the need for excessive oil.

Multiple Cooking Functions: The appliance offers various settings, including air fry, roast, bake, reheat, and dehydrate, providing versatility for different cooking needs.

Digital Controls: An intuitive digital touchscreen allows users to select cooking functions, adjust temperature and time, and monitor progress easily.

Non-Stick Basket and Crisper Plate: The removable, non-stick components facilitate easy cleaning and prevent food from sticking during cooking.

Large Capacity: With a 5.2-litre (5.5-quart) capacity, it can accommodate meals for families or gatherings, reducing the need for multiple cooking batches.

Energy Efficiency: The appliance cooks food faster than traditional methods, reducing energy consumption and cooking time.

Safety Features: Built-in safety mechanisms, such as automatic shut-off and cool-touch handles, ensure safe operation during use.

By integrating these features, the Ninja Air Fryer Max provides a convenient and efficient cooking experience, allowing users to prepare a wide range of dishes with minimal oil and effort.

Benefits of Using it

Healthier Cooking
One of the primary benefits of using the Ninja Air Fryer Max is its ability to cook food with little to no oil. This significantly reduces the fat content in your meals, allowing you to enjoy crispy, tasty dishes while maintaining a healthier lifestyle. Whether you're air frying, roasting, or baking, you can cook your favourite foods in a much healthier way than traditional frying methods.

Max Crisp Technology for Faster Cooking
The Ninja Air Fryer Max uses advanced Max Crisp Technology that allows it to reach a higher temperature of up to 240°C (475°F), ensuring faster cooking times. This means you can enjoy crispy, delicious food without having to wait long, perfect for busy households or when you're looking for a quick meal option. The high heat also helps lock in moisture, resulting in tender and juicy food.

Versatile Cooking Functions
This air fryer isn't limited to just frying. It offers a range of functions, including air frying, roasting, baking, reheating, and dehydrating. This versatility means you can prepare a wide variety of dishes, from crispy chicken wings and roasted vegetables to baked goods and dried fruits, all in one appliance. The ability to switch between functions makes it ideal for various cooking needs.

Generous Capacity
With a 5.2-litre (5.5-quart) capacity, the Ninja Air Fryer Max is perfect for cooking larger portions of food, making it ideal for families or entertaining guests. You can cook up to 1.4 kg (3 lbs) of chicken wings or a whole 1.8 kg (4 lbs) chicken, which saves you time and effort. It's large enough to prepare meals for multiple people in one go, yet still compact enough to fit on your kitchen countertop.

Fundamentals of Ninja Air Fryer Max

User-Friendly Digital Display
The Ninja Air Fryer Max comes with an intuitive digital touchscreen that makes it easy to adjust settings, choose cooking functions, and monitor your cooking progress. The clear, easy-to-read display ensures that you can cook with confidence, even if you're new to air frying. The presets for common foods make it even easier to cook the perfect meal with just the touch of a button.

Crispy Results Every Time
Thanks to the powerful air circulation and Max Crisp Technology, the Ninja Air Fryer Max delivers crispy, golden results every time, without the need for excessive oil. Whether you're cooking frozen food, fresh vegetables, or your favourite comfort foods, the air fryer ensures a crispy texture on the outside, while keeping the inside juicy and tender.

Quick and Efficient Cooking
The high temperature capabilities and rapid air circulation of the Ninja Air Fryer Max ensure that your food cooks faster than traditional methods. For example, frozen fries can be cooked in just 20 minutes, saving you time and effort compared to conventional frying or oven baking. The speed of cooking makes it perfect for busy families or anyone looking to prepare meals in a fraction of the time.

Easier Clean-Up
Cleaning after cooking can be a hassle, but the Ninja Air Fryer Max makes it easy. The non-stick, dishwasher-safe basket and crisper plate ensure that food residue doesn't stick, making cleaning a breeze. Simply remove the basket and crisper plate after use, and either wash them by hand or pop them into the dishwasher for a thorough clean.

Energy Efficient
The Ninja Air Fryer Max is more energy-efficient than traditional ovens. Since it cooks faster and requires less power to heat up, it consumes less electricity overall. This makes it a more economical choice for daily cooking, especially for quick meals or reheating leftovers. The reduced cooking time also means less heat is generated, making it ideal for hot summer days when you don't want to heat up the kitchen.

Compact Design for Easy Storage
Despite its large cooking capacity, the Ninja Air Fryer Max is designed with a compact footprint, making it easy to store when not in use. Its sleek, modern design means it can fit easily into any kitchen space, and the removable parts make it easy to store away. This is particularly useful for those with limited kitchen space who still want the power of a full-sized air fryer.

Before First Use

Remove All Packaging Material: Carefully remove and dispose of all packaging materials, including promotional labels, stickers, and tape. Ensure that no packaging material is left on the unit to maintain a clean and functional appliance.

Remove Accessories and Read the Manual: Take out all the accessories included with the appliance. It is important to read the user manual thoroughly before operating the unit. Pay close attention to the operational instructions, safety warnings, and essential safeguards to ensure safe and efficient use, preventing any potential injuries or damage to property.

Clean the Accessories: Wash all accessories such as the drawer and crisper plate with hot, soapy water. Make sure to rinse them thoroughly to remove any soap residue. Dry the accessories completely with a clean towel or air dry before reassembling them for use. Important Note: Never attempt to clean the main unit in the dishwasher, as this could damage the appliance. Always clean the unit using a damp cloth to

wipe the exterior and avoid any water getting into the internal components.

Ensure Adequate Space for Ventilation: When setting up the appliance for use, make sure there is sufficient space around it. Keep at least 6 inches (15 cm) of clearance above and around the unit. This space is essential for proper air circulation, which helps prevent overheating and ensures optimal performance during operation.

Understanding the Control Panel

Function Buttons

1. MAX CRISP: This function is designed to give frozen foods an extra level of crispiness and crunch without the need for much oil. It uses high heat to achieve a crispy exterior while keeping the inside tender and moist. Ideal for frozen foods like fries, chicken wings, and spring rolls.

2. AIR FRY: Similar to the MAX CRISP function, Air Fry uses rapid hot air circulation to cook food to a golden crisp texture with little to no oil. It's perfect for making healthier versions of your favourite fried foods such as chips, chicken, and vegetables.

3. ROAST: The Roast function allows the unit to act as a mini oven, ideal for roasting tender meats, vegetables, and even baked potatoes. It distributes heat evenly, ensuring a delicious caramelised exterior while keeping the inside juicy and tender.

4. BAKE: Use the Bake function to create delicious baked treats and desserts. Whether you're baking cakes, cookies, or pastries, this function provides even heat for perfectly baked goods every time.

5. REHEAT: The Reheat function gently warms leftovers, ensuring they're heated through without losing their crispy texture. Whether it's pizza, fries, or other foods, you can bring them back to life with a fresh, crispy finish.

6. DEHYDRATE: This function is great for dehydrating fruits, vegetables, meats, and other foods to make healthy snacks like dried fruits, beef jerky, or even homemade chips. It uses low heat for long periods to dry out the moisture from the food, preserving the flavours and nutrients.

Operating Buttons

1. TEMP Arrows: The up and down temperature arrows allow you to adjust the cooking temperature for any function, except for MAX CRISP, either before or during cooking. This gives you full control over the cooking process, whether you want a higher temperature for crisping or a lower one for slow cooking.

2. TIME Arrows: These up and down arrows allow you to set the cooking time. You can adjust the time before or during cooking, giving you flexibility to manage your cooking process as it progresses.

3. START/STOP Button: Once you've selected your desired cooking time and temperature, press the Start/Stop button to begin cooking. If you need to stop cooking for any reason, press the button again to halt the process.

4. POWER Button: The Power button is used to turn off the unit, stopping all cooking modes. Pressing this button will immediately shut down the appliance and stop all operations, ensuring safety and energy efficiency when not in use.

These buttons and functions make the Ninja Air Fryer Max easy to operate while providing a wide variety of cooking options to suit your needs. (NOTE: After 10 minutes with no interaction with the control panel, the unit will enter standby mode. The Power button will be dimly lit.)

Using All Functions

Max Crisp
1. Place the crisper plate in the upper position of the drawer to allow for optimal airflow and crisping.
2. Press the MAX CRISP button to select this function. The temperature is fixed and cannot be adjusted for this function.
3. Set the desired cooking time using the TIME button.
4. Add your ingredients to the drawer, ensuring they are evenly spread out for optimal cooking results.
5. Insert the drawer into the unit and press START/STOP to begin cooking.
6. When the cooking time ends, the unit will beep, and END will appear on the control panel. Carefully remove the food by tipping it out of the drawer or using oven gloves or silicone-tipped tongs to avoid burns.

Air Fry
1. Place the crisper plate in the lower position of the drawer, which is ideal for air frying.
2. Press the AIR FRY button to select the function.
3. Adjust the temperature using the TEMP buttons and set the cooking time with the TIME buttons.
4. Add the ingredients to the drawer, ensuring they are not overcrowded for even air circulation.
5. Insert the drawer into the unit and press START/STOP to begin cooking.
6. Once the cooking is complete, the unit will beep, and END will appear on the control panel. Remove the ingredients carefully, either by tipping them out or using oven gloves or silicone-tipped tongs.

Roast
1. Optionally, place the crisper plate in the lower position for roasting, or use it without depending on your preference.
2. Press the ROAST button to select this function.
3. Set the desired temperature and cooking time using the TEMP and TIME buttons.
4. Place the ingredients in the drawer, ensuring they are spread evenly for optimal roasting.

5. Insert the drawer into the unit and press START/STOP to begin.
6. When the cooking time ends, the unit will beep, and END will be displayed. Remove the food using oven gloves or silicone-tipped tongs.

Bake
1. For baking, place the crisper plate in the lower position in the drawer if desired.
2. Select the BAKE function by pressing the BAKE button.
3. Set your preferred temperature and time using the TEMP and TIME buttons.
4. Place the ingredients in the drawer, ensuring they are evenly distributed for even baking.
5. Press START/STOP to begin baking.
6. Once the cooking time is up, the unit will beep, and END will appear on the display. Carefully remove the baked items from the drawer using oven gloves or silicone-tipped tongs.

Reheat
1. For reheating leftovers, place the crisper plate in the lower position in the drawer.
2. Press the REHEAT button to select this function.
3. Adjust the temperature and time according to your preference using the TEMP and TIME buttons.
4. Add the leftovers to the drawer, ensuring they are spread evenly for even reheating.
5. Press START/STOP to begin the reheating process.
6. When the cooking time is complete, the unit will beep, and END will appear. Remove the food with care, using oven gloves or silicone-tipped tongs to avoid burns.

Dehydrate
1. Place the first layer of ingredients at the bottom of the drawer. Then place the crisper plate in the lower position. Add a second layer of ingredients on top of the crisper plate for an even dehydration process.
2. Insert the drawer into the unit.
3. Press the DEHYDRATE button to select this function.
4. Adjust the temperature and time as per the recipe or your preference using the TEMP and TIME buttons.
5. Press START/STOP to begin dehydrating.
6. Once the dehydration process is complete, the unit will beep, and END will appear on the control panel. Remove the dehydrated food carefully by tipping it out or using silicone-tipped tongs.

Tips for Using Accessories

The Ninja Air Fryer Max comes with several essential accessories that can significantly enhance your cooking experience. Understanding how to use these accessories properly will help you achieve the best results. Here are some key tips for using each accessory effectively:

Crisper Plate

Optimal Placement: The crisper plate should be placed in the lower position within the drawer when air frying. This ensures that the food is elevated, allowing the hot air to circulate evenly around the ingredients, resulting in a crispier finish.

For Even Cooking: To avoid uneven cooking, always ensure that the food is arranged in a single layer on the crisper plate, with no overlapping. If cooking larger batches, consider shaking the food halfway through cooking to ensure even crisping on all sides.

Use with Vegetables and Potatoes: The crisper plate is ideal for foods like chips, fries, and vegetables. The elevated design ensures that these foods cook evenly and become crispy, as they're exposed to consistent airflow.

Removable Splatter Shield

Prevent Grease Splattering: The splatter shield is designed to reduce grease and splatter, keeping your cooking area cleaner. It is especially useful when cooking items like bacon or sausages that tend to release grease during cooking.

Ensure Proper Placement: Ensure that the splatter shield is properly fitted inside the cooking pot or the air fryer drawer. This accessory helps to create a barrier between the hot air and the food, reducing the risk of splattering.

Grill Plate

Use for Grilling and Searing: The grill plate is perfect for grilling meats like steaks, burgers, and fish, providing those beautiful charred marks and crispy texture. It also helps with searing, locking in the flavour and juices of the food.

Preheat the Grill Plate: Always preheat the grill plate for a few minutes before adding food to ensure that it's hot enough to sear the food properly.

Even Cooking: Like the other accessories, arrange the food on the grill plate in a single layer to allow for even cooking. Avoid overcrowding the plate, as this can lead to uneven cooking and prevent the grill marks from forming.

Reversible Rack (if available)

Two Cooking Heights: The reversible rack allows you to adjust the height of the food within the cooking chamber. Use the lower setting for foods that need more space for airflow (such as fries or chicken wings) and the upper setting for smaller items like sausages or vegetables that don't need as much room.

Multi-Level Cooking: The rack can also be used for multi-level cooking, allowing you to cook different foods at once, saving time and improving efficiency. However, ensure that the food is properly arranged to prevent it from blocking airflow to the food on the lower level.

Use Silicone Utensils

Gentle on Surfaces: Always use silicone-tipped tongs or utensils when handling food in the basket or pot. This prevents scratches or damage to the non-stick surfaces of your accessories.

Easy Handling: Silicone utensils are gentle on the cooking accessories and will help you manoeuvre food without disturbing the cooking process or damaging your cookware.

Proper Storage
Store Accessories Safely: When not in use, store the accessories in a dry and cool place. Make sure they're not in contact with any sharp objects to avoid scratches. For easy access, consider keeping them in a storage container or drawer dedicated to air fryer accessories.

Food Safety Tips
Check Food Temperature: Whether using the crisper plate, cooking pot, or grill plate, always check the internal temperature of your food to ensure it's safely cooked. Use a food thermometer to verify that meats are cooked to their proper temperature before serving.
Avoid Using Non-Compatible Accessories: Only use accessories that are specifically designed for the Ninja Air Fryer Max. Using non-approved accessories can compromise performance and potentially damage the unit.

Cleaning the Accessories
After Every Use: Clean your accessories after every use to prevent any food residue buildup. Most accessories are dishwasher-safe, but it's always best to refer to the manufacturer's instructions for specific cleaning recommendations.
Soaking for Stubborn Residue: If any food is stuck to the accessories, soak them in warm, soapy water before scrubbing gently. This will help to loosen any stubborn food particles without damaging the surface.

By using the accessories properly, you can maximise the versatility of the Ninja Air Fryer Max and make the most of every cooking experience. With the right accessories, you can air fry, bake, grill, roast, dehydrate, and much more – all with the help of these essential tools.

Helpful Cooking Tips

Even Layering for Consistent Browning: To ensure uniform browning, arrange the ingredients in a single, even layer at the bottom of the drawer. Avoid overlapping. If ingredients overlap, shake the contents halfway through the cooking time to promote even cooking.
Adjusting Cook Time and Temperature: The cook time and temperature can be modified at any point during cooking. Simply press the up or down TIME and TEMP arrows to adjust the settings as needed to suit your preferences.
Converting Oven Recipes: When adapting conventional oven recipes for the air fryer, it's recommended to reduce the temperature by 10°C. Check the food frequently to prevent overcooking and to ensure it reaches the desired result.
Preventing Lightweight Foods from Blowing Around: Sometimes, the air fryer fan may cause lightweight items, like

Fundamentals of Ninja Air Fryer Max

the top slice of bread on a sandwich, to move around. Secure such foods with cocktail sticks or toothpicks to hold them in place and prevent movement.

Crisper Plate for Even Cooking: The crisper plate in the drawer elevates the ingredients, allowing hot air to circulate underneath and around them. This helps to achieve even, crispy results, particularly for items like fries and vegetables.

Starting Cooking Immediately: Once you have selected a cooking function, you can begin cooking straight away by pressing the START/STOP button. The unit will automatically run at its default temperature and time settings, but these can be adjusted as needed.

Avoid Overcooking by Removing Food Promptly: To ensure the best results, remove the food as soon as the cooking time is up to prevent overcooking. The longer food sits in the air fryer, the more it will continue to cook due to residual heat.

Using Oil for Vegetables and Potatoes: For optimal results, especially with fresh vegetables and potatoes, use at least 1 tablespoon of oil. You can adjust the amount of oil based on how crispy you prefer your food.

Monitoring Cooking Progress: Regularly check the food during cooking to ensure it reaches the desired level of crispiness or browning. Use an instant-read thermometer to monitor the internal temperature of meats or dense foods. Once the desired result is achieved, remove the food promptly to avoid overcooking.

Cleaning and Caring

It is essential to clean the unit thoroughly after every use to maintain optimal performance and hygiene.

1. **Unplug the Unit:** Always unplug the unit from the wall socket before cleaning to ensure safety.
2. **Cleaning the Main Unit and Control Panel:** Use a damp cloth to wipe down the main unit and the control panel. Avoid using scouring pads, as they can damage the surface.
3. **Washing the Drawer and Crisper Plate:** Both the drawer and crisper plate are dishwasher-safe, making them easy to clean. Simply place them in the dishwasher for a thorough clean.
4. **Soaking for Stubborn Food Residue:** If food residue is stuck on the crisper plate or drawer, fill the sink with warm, soapy water and soak the parts for a while. After soaking, scrub gently to remove any remaining residue.
5. **Drying the Parts:** After cleaning, either air-dry the parts or use a towel to dry them thoroughly before reassembling the unit.

By following these steps, you will ensure that your Ninja Air Fryer Max remains in excellent condition for long-term use. Regular cleaning also helps to maintain the appliance's efficiency and ensures your food is cooked in a clean environment.

Frequently Asked Questions

1. Why won't the temperature go any higher?
The maximum temperature for the MAX CRISP function is 240°C. For all other functions, the maximum temperature is 210°C. If you're trying to exceed these limits, it won't be possible as they are the designated temperature ranges for optimal cooking.

2. When should I use MAX CRISP instead of Air Fry?
MAX CRISP is best used when cooking pre-packaged frozen foods, such as French fries or chicken nuggets, as it gives them a crispier texture. Air fry is a great alternative for fresh foods and cooking from scratch, but for frozen items, MAX CRISP ensures that extra crunch.

3. Do I need to defrost frozen foods before air frying?
Whether or not you need to defrost frozen food depends on the type of food. Always refer to the packaging instructions. Many frozen items, such as fries and chicken nuggets, are designed to be cooked from frozen.

4. How do I pause the countdown?
The countdown timer will automatically pause when you remove the drawer from the unit. If you need to pause the cooking manually, simply press the START/STOP button, which will stop the cooking process and reset the timer.

5. Is the drawer safe to put on my worktop?
The drawer will heat up during cooking, so it's important to exercise caution when handling it. Always place it on heat-safe surfaces, such as a countertop with a heat-resistant mat or a trivet.

6. How do I know when to use the crisper plate?
Use the crisper plate when you want your food to come out crispy. It elevates the food in the drawer, allowing air to circulate underneath, resulting in even cooking and a crisp texture.

7. My food didn't cook properly, what should I do?
Ensure that the drawer is fully inserted into the unit. For consistent browning, make sure the food is arranged in a single, even layer on the bottom of the drawer, avoiding overlap. Shake the ingredients during cooking to help them cook evenly. You can adjust the cooking time and temperature at any point during cooking by pressing the TIME or TEMP buttons and rotating the dial.

8. My food is overcooked, what went wrong?
To avoid overcooking, check the progress of your food throughout the cooking process. Remove the food as soon as it reaches the desired level of crispness. Always remove the food immediately when the timer finishes to prevent it from becoming overdone.

9. Why do some ingredients blow around when air frying?
The fan inside the air fryer can sometimes blow lightweight foods around. If this happens, secure loose items (like the top slice of a sandwich) with cocktail sticks to keep them in place.

10. Can I air fry fresh battered ingredients?
Yes, you can. However, for best results, make sure you coat your food properly before air frying. First coat the food with flour, then dip it in egg, and finish with bread crumbs. Press the breadcrumbs firmly so they stick. Loose breadcrumbs may be blown off by the air fryer's powerful fan.

11. Why is the unit beeping?
The unit beeps to indicate that the cooking function is complete. It's a sign that your food is ready to be served.

12. Why has the screen gone black?
If the screen turns black, it means the unit has entered standby mode. Simply press the power button to turn the unit back on and continue with your cooking or air frying.

4-Week Meal Plan

Week 1

Day 1:
Breakfast: Vegetable Breakfast Tacos
Lunch: Honey Roasted Baby Carrots
Snack: Air Fried Cheddar Sandwich
Dinner: Authentic Chicken Parmesan
Dessert: Bread Pudding with Cranberries and Raisins

Day 2:
Breakfast: Scrambled Eggs with Mushrooms
Lunch: Crispy Buffalo Cauliflower
Snack: Air Fried Stuffed Mushrooms
Dinner: Nutritious Cucumber and Salmon Salad
Dessert: Chocolate and Peanut Butter Tart

Day 3:
Breakfast: Cheesy Breakfast Sandwich
Lunch: Easy Sweet Potato Fries
Snack: Crispy Jalapeño Poppers
Dinner: Country-Style Barbecue Ribs
Dessert: Chocolate Lava Cake with Raspberry Sauce

Day 4:
Breakfast: Mixed Vegetable Hash
Lunch: Air Fryer Fried Green Tomatoes
Snack: Homemade Mozzarella Cheese Sticks
Dinner: Air Fryer Jerk Chicken Thighs
Dessert: Fluffy Gingerbread Cake

Day 5:
Breakfast: Cranberry Orange Muffin
Lunch: Chinese Vegetable Fried Rice
Snack: Crispy Potato Chips
Dinner: Crispy Coconut Shrimp
Dessert: Air Fryer Mixed Berry Pavlova

Day 6:
Breakfast: Crispy French Toast with Pecans
Lunch: Air-Fried Cheese Sandwich
Snack: Loaded Baked Potato Skins
Dinner: Spicy Pork Tenderloin with Avocado Lime Sauce
Dessert: Fresh Berry Cream Puffs

Day 7:
Breakfast: Savoury Baked Tofu
Lunch: Cheesy Rice Stuffed Peppers
Snack: Parmesan Dill Fried Pickles
Dinner: Glazed Ham Steaks with Sweet Potatoes
Dessert: Mini Chocolate Nut Pies

Week 2

Day 1:
Breakfast: Banana Walnut Breakfast Muffins
Lunch: Roasted Rosemary Red Potatoes
Snack: Bacon Wrapped Jalapeño Poppers
Dinner: Crispy Pickle-Brined Fried Chicken
Dessert: Air Fried Cinnamon Doughnut Bites

Day 2:
Breakfast: Italian Frittata with Tomato and Cheese
Lunch: Baked Sweet Potatoes with Honey Butter
Snack: Crispy Sweet Potato Chips
Dinner: Low-Carb Tuna Patties with Spicy Sriracha Sauce
Dessert: Baked Coconut Pie

Day 3:
Breakfast: Tofu Breakfast Sandwiches
Lunch: Air Fried Vegan Chimichanga
Snack: Parmesan Courgette Chips with Lemon Aioli
Dinner: Beef Lasagna Casserole
Dessert: Maple Pecan Squares

Day 4:
Breakfast: Easy Apple Fritters
Lunch: Cheesy Refried Bean Taquitos
Snack: Cinnamon Spiced Nuts
Dinner: Greek Turkey Burgers with Tzatziki Sauce
Dessert: Chocolate Chip Pecan Biscotti

Day 5:
Breakfast: Savoury Baked Tofu
Lunch: Tamale Pie with Cornmeal Crust
Snack: Tomato and Spinach Stuffed Portobello Mushrooms
Dinner: Crispy Fish Sticks with Tartar Sauce
Dessert: Tasty Chocolate Soufflés

Day 6:
Breakfast: Brown Sugar Streusel Donuts
Lunch: Sesame Crusted Tofu Steaks
Snack: Crispy Kale Chips
Dinner: Beef Meatballs and Spaghetti Zoodles
Dessert: Keto Almond Flour Cinnamon Rolls

Day 7:
Breakfast: Cranberry Oatmeal Muffins
Lunch: Honey Roasted Baby Carrots
Snack: Greek Street Taco Hand Pies
Dinner: Crispy Chinese Five-Spice Pork Belly
Dessert: Bread Pudding with Cranberries and Raisins

Week 3

Day 1:
Breakfast: Cheesy German Apple Pancakes
Lunch: Crispy Buffalo Cauliflower
Snack: Jalapeño Cheese Balls
Dinner: Spinach and Feta Chicken Meatballs
Dessert: Chocolate and Peanut Butter Tart

Day 2:
Breakfast: Scrambled Eggs with Mushrooms
Lunch: Easy Sweet Potato Fries
Snack: Air Fried Cheddar Sandwich
Dinner: Crispy Buttermilk Catfish Strips
Dessert: Chocolate Lava Cake with Raspberry Sauce

Day 3:
Breakfast: Mixed Vegetable Hash
Lunch: Air Fryer Fried Green Tomatoes
Snack: Crispy Jalapeño Poppers
Dinner: Air-Fried Rib Eye Steaks with Horseradish Cream
Dessert: Air Fryer Mixed Berry Pavlova

Day 4:
Breakfast: Vegetable Breakfast Tacos
Lunch: Roasted Rosemary Red Potatoes
Snack: Homemade Mozzarella Cheese Sticks
Dinner: Spicy Black Bean Turkey Burgers with Avocado Spread
Dessert: Fluffy Gingerbread Cake

Day 5:
Breakfast: Cranberry Orange Muffin
Lunch: Air-Fried Cheese Sandwich
Snack: Crispy Potato Chips
Dinner: Delicious Bang Bang Shrimp
Dessert: Mini Peanut Butter Tarts

Day 6:
Breakfast: Savoury Baked Tofu
Lunch: Chinese Vegetable Fried Rice
Snack: Loaded Baked Potato Skins
Dinner: Guacamole Bacon Burgers
Dessert: Fresh Berry Cream Puffs

Day 7:
Breakfast: Crispy French Toast with Pecans
Lunch: Cheesy Rice Stuffed Peppers
Snack: Air Fried Stuffed Mushrooms
Dinner: Honey Lemon Roasted Pork Loin
Dessert: Mini Chocolate Nut Pies

Week 4

Day 1:
Breakfast: Cheesy Breakfast Sandwich
Lunch: Baked Sweet Potatoes with Honey Butter
Snack: Parmesan Dill Fried Pickles
Dinner: Classic Nashville Hot Chicken
Dessert: Baked Coconut Pie

Day 2:
Breakfast: Easy Apple Fritters
Lunch: Air Fried Vegan Chimichanga
Snack: Greek Street Taco Hand Pies
Dinner: Hearty Crab Stuffed Salmon Roast
Dessert: Air Fried Cinnamon Doughnut Bites

Day 3:
Breakfast: Banana Walnut Breakfast Muffins
Lunch: Tamale Pie with Cornmeal Crust
Snack: Bacon Wrapped Jalapeño Poppers
Dinner: Blue Cheese and Steak Salad with Balsamic Vinaigrette
Dessert: Maple Pecan Squares

Day 4:
Breakfast: Italian Frittata with Tomato and Cheese
Lunch: Cheesy Refried Bean Taquitos
Snack: Crispy Sweet Potato Chips
Dinner: Thai Courgette Turkey Meatballs
Dessert: Chocolate Chip Pecan Biscotti

Day 5:
Breakfast: Brown Sugar Streusel Donuts
Lunch: Tomato and Spinach Stuffed Portobello Mushrooms
Snack: Parmesan Courgette Chips with Lemon Aioli
Dinner: Blackened Shrimp Tacos with Coleslaw
Dessert: Tasty Chocolate Soufflés

Day 6:
Breakfast: Cranberry Oatmeal Muffins
Lunch: Sesame Crusted Tofu Steaks
Snack: Cinnamon Spiced Nuts
Dinner: Marinated Steak Tips with Mushrooms
Dessert: Mini Peanut Butter Tarts

Day 7:
Breakfast: Cheesy German Apple Pancakes
Lunch: Honey Roasted Baby Carrots
Snack: Crispy Kale Chips
Dinner: Crispy Breaded Pork Chops
Dessert: Keto Almond Flour Cinnamon Rolls

Chapter 1 Breakfast

13	Vegetable Breakfast Tacos	16	Easy Apple Fritters
13	Savoury Baked Tofu	17	Brown Sugar Streusel Donuts
14	Cheesy Breakfast Sandwich	17	Cranberry Oatmeal Muffins
14	Tofu Breakfast Sandwiches	18	Cheesy German Apple Pancakes
15	Crispy French Toast with Pecans	18	Scrambled Eggs with Mushrooms
15	Cranberry Orange Muffin	19	Mixed Vegetable Hash
16	Banana Walnut Breakfast Muffins	19	Italian Frittata with Tomato and Cheese

Vegetable Breakfast Tacos

⏱ **Prep Time: 5 minutes** 🍲 **Cook: 12 minutes** ⊛ **Serves: 3**

Cooking oil spray (sunflower, safflower, or refined coconut)
1 small courgette, cut ¼-inch-thick slices or cubes
1 small-medium yellow onion, cut ½-inch slices
¼ teaspoon garlic granules
⅛ teaspoon sea salt
Freshly ground black pepper
1 (425g) can vegan refried beans
6 corn tortillas
Fresh salsa of your choice
1 avocado, cut into slices or cubes, or fresh guacamole

1. Insert the crisper plate in the drawer in the lower position and spray the crisper plate with the oil. Add the courgette and onion to the drawer and spray with more oil and sprinkle evenly with the garlic, salt, and pepper to taste. Insert the drawer into the unit. 2. Select ROAST, set the temperature to 200°C and set the time for 6 minutes. Select START/STOP to begin cooking. 3. Remove, shake or stir well, and cook for another 6 minutes, or until the veggies are nicely browned and tender. 4. In a small pan, warm the refried beans over low heat. Stir often. Once to temperature, remove from the heat and set aside. 5. To prepare the tortillas, sprinkle them individually with a little water, then place in a hot skillet in a single layer, turning over as each side becomes hot. 6. Make the breakfast tacos by placing a corn tortilla on your plate and filling it with beans, roasted vegetables, salsa, and avocado slices.

Savoury Baked Tofu

⏱ **Prep Time: 10 minutes** 🍲 **Cook: 14 minutes** ⊛ **Serves: 4**

1 (225g) package firm or extra-firm tofu
4 teaspoons tamari or shoyu
1 teaspoons onion granules
½ teaspoon garlic granules
½ teaspoon turmeric powder
¼ teaspoon freshly ground black pepper
2 tablespoons nutritional yeast
1 teaspoon dried rosemary
1 teaspoon dried dill
2 teaspoons arrowroot (or cornstarch)
2 teaspoons neutral-flavoured oil (such as sunflower, safflower, or melted refined coconut)
Cooking oil spray (sunflower, safflower, or refined coconut)

1. Cut the tofu into slices and press out the excess water. 2. Cut the slices into ½-inch cubes and place in a bowl. Sprinkle with the tamari and toss gently to coat. Set aside for a few minutes. 3. Toss the tofu again and then add the onion, garlic, turmeric, and pepper. Gently toss to thoroughly coat. 4. Add the nutritional yeast, rosemary, dill, and arrowroot. Toss gently to coat. 5. Finally, drizzle with the oil and toss one last time. 6. Insert the crisper plate in the drawer in the lower position and spray the crisper plate with the oil. Place the tofu on the crisper plate and insert the drawer into the unit. 7. Select BAKE, set the temperature to 200°C and set the time for 7 minutes. Select START/STOP to begin cooking. 8. Remove, shake gently (so that the tofu cooks evenly), and cook for another 7 minutes, or until the tofu is crisp and browned. 9. When done, serve and enjoy.

Chapter 1 Breakfast | 13

Cheesy Breakfast Sandwich

⏰ **Prep Time: 15 minutes** 🍲 **Cook: 13 minutes** 🍃 **Serves: 2**

1 (225g) package firm or extra-firm tofu, thinly sliced into rectangles or squares
2 teaspoons nutritional yeast, divided
¼ teaspoon sea salt, divided
⅛ teaspoon freshly ground black pepper, divided
Cooking oil spray (sunflower, safflower, or refined coconut)
4 slices bread
Cheesy sauce
Vegan tempeh bacon (optional)
Vegan mayo, your choice (optional)
Leaf lettuce, dill pickles, and thinly sliced red onion (optional)

1. Place the tofu slices in a single layer on a plate and sprinkle evenly with 1 teaspoon nutritional yeast, ⅛ teaspoon salt, and half of teaspoon pepper. Turn over and sprinkle the remaining yeast, salt, and pepper on top. 2. Insert the crisper plate in the drawer in the lower position and spray the crisper plate with the oil. Place the tofu pieces in a single layer on the crisper plate and spray the tops with the oil. 3. Select BAKE, set the temperature to 200°C and set the time for 7 minutes. Select START/STOP to begin cooking. 4. While the tofu is cooking, prepare your optional additions. 5. After the tofu has cooked for 7 minutes, flip each piece over and spray again with the oil. Bake for another 6 minutes, or until golden and lightly crisp. 6. Toast the bread and top with the tofu slices, cheesy sauce, vegan meat (if using), and any additional toppings. Devour immediately.

Tofu Breakfast Sandwiches

⏰ **Prep Time: 5 minutes** 🍲 **Cook: 6 minutes** 🍃 **Serves: 4**

About 1 tsp (5g) Breakfast Seasoning Mix
1 (395g]) package extra-firm tofu, pressed and cut into 4 rectangles
4 vegan whole wheat English muffins (or use gluten-free)
Vegan cheese slices or spread (optional)
Toppings: lettuce, tomato, avocado, cucumbers, red onion, spinach, etc.

1. Rub the breakfast seasoning mix on the 4 tofu rectangles. Be sure to do the front, back and edges. 2. Insert the crisper plate in the drawer in the lower position and place the tofu rectangles in the drawer and place English muffins on either side. You may need to do this in batches. Insert the drawer into the unit. 3. Select AIR FRY, set the temperature to 165°C and set the time to 3 minutes. Select START/STOP to begin cooking. 4. When the time is up, flip the tofu and the English muffin halves over. Repeat for an additional 3 minutes. 5. Remove the English muffins and pile on your toppings!

14 | Chapter 1 Breakfast

Crispy French Toast with Pecans

⏰ **Prep Time:** 10 minutes 🍲 **Cook:** 6 minutes 🍽 **Serves:** 4

85g rolled oats
115g pecans, or nut of your choice
2 tbsp (15g) ground flax seed
1 tsp (5g) ground cinnamon
180ml nondairy milk (plain or vanilla)
8 slices whole-grain vegan bread, regular or cinnamon raisin (use gluten-free bread)
Maple syrup, for serving

1. Make the topping by adding the oats, flax seed, nuts, and cinnamon to your food processor and pulsing until it looks similar to breadcrumbs. Do not overblend. Pour the topping into a shallow pan that's large enough to dip your bread slices in. 2. Add the nondairy milk to a second container and then soak one or two pieces of the bread for about 5 seconds, turn and soak the other side. You don't want to leave it long enough to become mushy. If your bread is fresh and moist, it may take even less time. 3. Insert the crisper plate in the drawer in the lower position, place the bread in the drawer without overlapping, and insert the drawer into the unit. 4. Select AIR FRY, set the temperature to 180°C and set the time to 3 minutes. Select START/STOP to begin cooking. 5. Flip the bread and cook for another 3 minutes. Repeat until all the bread is coated and cooked. 6. Serve topped with the maple syrup.

Cranberry Orange Muffin

⏰ **Prep Time:** 5 minutes 🍲 **Cook:** 15 minutes 🍽 **Serves:** 1

25g whole wheat pastry flour (use oat flour)
¼ tsp baking powder
Pinch salt
3 tbsp (45ml) orange juice (or unsweetened nondairy milk plus ¼ tsp orange extract)
1 tbsp (15g) brown or coconut sugar, or sweetener of choice to taste
2 tbsp (15g) dried cranberries
2 tbsp (15g) chopped nuts (optional)
1 tsp (5ml) mild oil (use applesauce or mashed banana)

1. Oil an oven-safe mug (use a single-serving-size nonstick pan to keep it oil-free). 2. Add the flour, baking powder, and salt and mix well with a fork. It's important to mix well so that the baking powder is evenly distributed. 3. Next add the orange juice, sugar, cranberries, nuts and oil and mix again. 4. Insert the crisper plate in the drawer in the lower position, place the mug in the drawer, and insert the drawer into the unit. 5. Select BAKE, set the temperature to 180°C and set the time for 15 minutes. Select START/STOP to begin cooking. Check with a fork to make sure the middle is cooked. If not, cook 5 minutes more. 6. When done, serve and enjoy.

Chapter 1 Breakfast | 15

Banana Walnut Breakfast Muffins

⏲ **Prep Time: 10 minutes** 🍳 **Cook: 10 minutes** 🍽 **Serves: 5**

Dry Ingredients:
50g whole wheat pastry flour (use gluten-free baking blend)
55g brown sugar (or sweetener of choice, to taste)
30g chopped pecans or vegan mini chocolate chips
2 tsp (5g) ground flax seed
½ tsp cinnamon
⅛ tsp baking powder
⅛ tsp baking soda
⅛ tsp salt
Pinch nutmeg (optional)

Wet Ingredients:
z small banana (100g), mashed
60ml aquafaba
2 tbsp (30ml) mild oil (use applesauce or extra mashed banana)
½ tsp vanilla extract

1. Mix the dry ingredients together in a bowl. Then mix the wet ingredients in a large measuring cup. Add the wet ingredients to the dry ingredients and mix well. 2. Either spray some oil in 5 small ramekins or use individual silicone muffin cups and line with the cupcake papers to keep it completely oil-free. Divide the batter among the ramekins. 3. Insert the crisper plate in the drawer in the lower position, place the ramekins in the drawer, and insert the drawer into the unit. 4. Select AIR FRY, set the temperature to 175°C and set the time to 10 minutes. Select START/STOP to begin cooking. 5. If the middle is not completely set, or if a knife doesn't come out clean when stuck in the middle, cook for another 5 minutes. The time may vary depending on the size ramekins and your particular air fryer. 6. When done, serve and enjoy.

Easy Apple Fritters

⏲ **Prep Time: 15 minutes** 🍳 **Cook: 10 minutes** 🍽 **Serves: 4**

90g all-purpose flour
2 tablespoons brown sugar
1 teaspoon baking powder
¼ teaspoon sea salt
½ teaspoon cinnamon
60ml 2% milk
1 large egg
3 teaspoons freshly squeezed orange juice, divided
1 Granny Smith apple, peeled, cored, and diced
3 tablespoons butter, melted, divided
120g powdered sugar
1 teaspoon vanilla
2 teaspoons grated orange zest

1. In a medium bowl, combine the flour, brown sugar, salt, baking powder, and cinnamon and mix well. 2. In a small bowl, whisk together the milk, egg, and 2 teaspoons of orange juice until combined. Stir this into the flour mixture. 3. Fold in the diced apples until they are evenly distributed. 4. Insert the crisper plate in the drawer in the lower position and line the drawer with parchment paper. 5. Depending on the size of your air fryer, drop two ¼-cup measures of the fritter mixture onto the parchment paper, 1½ inches apart. Drizzle each fritter with ½ tablespoon of melted butter. Insert the drawer into the unit. 6. Select AIR FRY, set the temperature to 175°C and set the time to 7 minutes. Select START/STOP to begin cooking. Air fry the fritters for 7 to 10 minutes or until they are golden brown and set. 7. Remove from the drawer and place on a cooling rack. 8. In a small bowl, combine the remaining 2 tablespoons of butter, remaining 1 teaspoon of orange juice, powdered sugar, and vanilla and blend well. Drizzle over the warm fritters. Sprinkle with the orange zest and serve.

Brown Sugar Streusel Donuts

⏰ Prep Time: 15 minutes 🍲 Cook: 6 minutes 📑 Serves: 6

120g plus 2 tablespoons all-purpose flour, divided, plus additional to dust the work surface
5 tablespoons dark brown sugar, divided
1 teaspoon baking powder
Pinch sea salt
60ml whole milk
1 large egg, yolk and white separated
3 tablespoons granulated sugar
½ teaspoon ground cinnamon
55g butter, melted
Cooking oil spray

1. In a medium bowl, combine 120g of flour, 2 tablespoons of brown sugar, the baking powder, and salt and mix well. 2. In a small bowl, whisk together the milk and egg yolk. Add the milk mixture to the flour mixture and mix just until a dough forms. 3. In another small bowl, combine the remaining 3 tablespoons of brown sugar, cinnamon, granulated sugar, remaining 2 tablespoons of flour, and butter and mix until a crumbly streusel forms Set aside. 4. Dust the work surface with some flour. Turn the dough out onto the surface and pat it to ⅓-inch thickness. Cut out 6 rounds with a 3-inch cookie cutter. We'll skip the donut holes so we can have more streusel on top. 5. Beat the egg white until frothy in a small bowl, then brush the tops of the rounds with some of the egg white. 6. Sprinkle each dough round with some of the streusel topping, patting the topping onto the dough so it sticks. 7. Cut two pieces of parchment paper to fit in your air fryer drawer. 8. Insert the crisper plate in the drawer in the lower position. Place a parchment paper round into the drawer and add the donuts, three at a time, depending on the size of your air fryer. Spray the tops with cooking oil. Insert the drawer into the unit. 9. Select AIR FRY, set the temperature to 175°C and set the time to 4 minutes. Select START/STOP to begin cooking. Air fry the donuts for 4 to 6 minutes or until they are light golden brown. 10. Remove the donuts and let cool on a wire rack. Remove and discard the parchment paper and replace with a fresh round. Air fry the remaining donuts. 11. When done, serve and enjoy.

Cranberry Oatmeal Muffins

⏰ Prep Time: 15 minutes 🍲 Cook: 14 minutes 📑 Serves: 4

60g all-purpose flour
2 tablespoons whole-wheat flour
½ teaspoon baking powder
2 tablespoons brown sugar
3 tablespoons quick-cooking oats
Pinch sea salt
1 large egg
60ml whole milk
1 teaspoon vanilla
2 tablespoons vegetable oil
40g dried cranberries
Nonstick baking spray containing flour

1. In a medium bowl, combine the all-purpose flour, whole-wheat flours, brown sugar, oats, baking powder, and salt and mix. 2. In a small bowl or a measuring cup, beat together the egg, vanilla, milk, and oil until combined. 3. Add the egg mixture to the dry ingredients all at once and stir just until combined. 4. Stir in the cranberries. 5. Spray four silicone muffin cups with the baking spray. Divide the batter among them, filling each two-thirds full. 6. Insert the crisper plate in the drawer in the lower position, place the muffin cups in the drawer, and insert the drawer into the unit. 7. Select BAKE, set the temperature to 160°C and set the time to 20 minutes. Select START/STOP to begin cooking. Bake for 12 to 14 minutes or until the muffins are browned and the tops spring back when you touch them lightly with your finger. 8. Let the muffins cool on a wire rack for 10 to 15 minutes before serving.

Cheesy German Apple Pancakes

⏲ **Prep Time: 15 minutes**   🍲 **Cook: 15 minutes**   ❖ **Serves: 3**

30g all-purpose flour
1 tablespoon granulated sugar
¼ teaspoon baking powder
2 large eggs
60ml 2% milk
55g small curd cottage cheese
2 tablespoons vegetable oil
2 tablespoons butter
2 tablespoons brown sugar
1 Granny Smith apple, peeled, cored, and sliced ⅛ inch thick
½ teaspoon cinnamon

1. In a medium bowl, combine the flour, sugar, and baking powder. 2. In a 2-cup glass measuring cup, whisk together the eggs, cottage cheese, milk, and oil until blended. 3. Add the egg mixture into the flour mixture and stir just until combined. Let stand while you prepare the apple mixture. 4. Put the butter in a round pan and place the pan in the drawer. Insert the drawer into the unit. 5. Select BAKE, set the temperature to 190°C and set the time for 1 minute. Select START/STOP to begin cooking. 6. Swirl the pan so the butter coats the bottom and ½ inch up the sides. Top evenly with the brown sugar and apples and sprinkle with the cinnamon. 7. Bake this mixture for 3 minutes or until the butter bubbles. Remove the pan. 8. Pour the batter over the apples. Return the pan to the drawer and bake for 9 to 11 minutes or until the batter is golden brown. 9. Cut into three wedges to serve.

Scrambled Eggs with Mushrooms

⏲ **Prep Time: 10 minutes**   🍲 **Cook: 16 minutes**   ❖ **Serves: 3**

2 tablespoons butter
155g sliced mushrooms
1 scallion, chopped
6 large eggs
2 tablespoons light cream
½ teaspoon dried thyme
½ teaspoon sea salt
⅛ teaspoon freshly ground black pepper

1. Place the butter in a round pan and put the pan in the drawer. Insert the drawer into the unit. 2. Select BAKE, set the temperature to 175°C and set the time for 1 minute. Select START/STOP to begin cooking. Melt the butter in the pan for 1 minute. 3. Remove the pan and add the mushrooms and scallions to the pan. 4. Return the pan to the drawer and bake for 5 minutes or until the mushrooms are lightly browned, shaking the pan after 3 minutes. 5. Meanwhile, in a medium bowl, whisk together the eggs, salt, thyme, light cream, and pepper until combined. 6. Remove the pan and pour the egg mixture into the pan. 7. Return to the pan to the drawer and bake for 8 to 10 minutes, stirring the egg mixture gently after 5 minutes, until the eggs are set. 8. When done, serve and enjoy.

| Chapter 1 Breakfast

Mixed Vegetable Hash

⏱ **Prep Time: 10 minutes** 🍲 **Cook: 30 minutes** ❖ **Serves: 4**

300g cubed potatoes (or turnips or rutabagas or a combo)
300g cubed sweet potatoes (or carrots or beets or a combo)
2 tsp (10ml) olive oil (omit)
1 tsp (5g) DIY Cajun seasoning blend (or use store-bought)
1 (425g to 565g) block super-firm or high-protein tofu cut into cubes or firm tofu pressed overnight (or use 360g cooked chickpeas)
2 tsp (5g) breakfast seasoning mix

1. Toss the potatoes and sweet potatoes in a large bowl with the olive oil, if using, and the Cajun seasoning. 2. Insert the crisper plate in the drawer in the lower position. Working in batches if necessary, arrange the potatoes and sweet potatoes in a single layer in the drawer. Insert the drawer into the unit. Select AIR FRY, set the temperature to 165°C and set the time to 10 minutes. Select START/STOP to begin cooking. 3. Shake the drawer, then cook 10 minutes more. 4. While the veggies are cooking, toss the tofu with the breakfast seasoning mix. Add on top of the veggies and cook on 200°C for 5 minutes, then shake and cook for 5 minutes more. 5. Serve with a side of ketchup and some sautéed greens.

Italian Frittata with Tomato and Cheese

⏱ **Prep Time: 15 minutes** 🍲 **Cook: 15 minutes** ❖ **Serves: 3**

1 tablespoon unsalted butter, at room temperature
4 large eggs, beaten
60g ricotta cheese
60g whole milk
1 teaspoon dried Italian seasoning
Pinch sea salt
2 scallions, chopped
1 garlic clove, minced
50g chopped cherry tomatoes, drained
120g shredded provolone cheese
25g grated Parmesan cheese

1. Grease a pan that fits your air fryer with the butter and set aside. 2. In a medium bowl, beat the eggs with the ricotta, Italian seasoning, milk, and salt. Pour this into the prepared pan. 3. Arrange the scallions, garlic, and tomatoes on the eggs. Top with the cheeses. 4. Place the pan in the drawer and insert the drawer into the unit. Select BAKE, set the temperature to 175°C and set the time for 12 minutes. Select START/STOP to begin cooking. Cook for 12 to 15 minutes or until the eggs are set and puffed. Serve.

Chapter 2 Vegetables and Sides

- 21 Honey Roasted Baby Carrots
- 21 Crispy Buffalo Cauliflower
- 21 Easy Sweet Potato Fries
- 22 Roasted Rosemary Red Potatoes
- 22 Cheesy Rice Stuffed Peppers
- 22 Chinese Vegetable Fried Rice
- 23 Air Fryer Fried Green Tomatoes
- 23 Baked Sweet Potatoes with Honey Butter
- 24 Air Fried Vegan Chimichanga
- 24 Cheesy Refried Bean Taquitos
- 25 Tomato and Spinach Stuffed Portobello Mushrooms
- 25 Sesame Crusted Tofu Steaks
- 26 Air-Fried Cheese Sandwich
- 26 Tamale Pie with Cornmeal Crust

Honey Roasted Baby Carrots

⏱ Prep Time: 5 minutes   🍳 Cook: 12 minutes   🍽 Serves: 4

720g baby carrots
1 tablespoon extra-virgin olive oil
1 tablespoon honey
Salt
Freshly ground black pepper
Fresh dill (optional)

1. In a large bowl, combine the carrots, olive oil, honey, salt, and pepper. Make sure that the carrots are thoroughly coated with oil. 2. Insert the crisper plate in the drawer in the lower position, place the carrots in the drawer, and insert the drawer into the unit. 3. Select ROAST, set the temperature to 200°C and set the time for 12 minutes. Select START/STOP to begin cooking. Cook until fork-tender. 4. Remove the drawer, pour the carrots into a bowl, sprinkle with dill, if desired, and serve.

Crispy Buffalo Cauliflower

⏱ Prep Time: 5 minutes   🍳 Cook: 13 minutes   🍽 Serves: 4

4 tablespoons (½ stick) unsalted butter, melted
70g buffalo wing sauce
430g cauliflower florets
110g panko bread crumbs

1. Insert the crisper plate in the drawer in the lower position and spray the crisper plate with the olive oil. 2. In a small bowl, combine the melted butter with the buffalo wing sauce. 3. Place the panko bread crumbs in a separate small bowl. 4. Dip the cauliflower in the sauce, making sure to coat the top of the cauliflower, and then dip the cauliflower in the panko. 5. Place the cauliflower into the greased drawer, being careful not to overcrowd them, and spray the cauliflower generously with the olive oil. Insert the drawer into the unit. 6. Select ROAST, set the temperature to 175°C and set the time for 7 minutes. Select START/STOP to begin cooking. 7. Using tongs, flip the cauliflower and spray generously with the olive oil. Continue to roast for another 6 minutes. 8. When done, serve and enjoy.

Easy Sweet Potato Fries

⏱ Prep Time: 5 minutes   🍳 Cook: 20-22 minutes   🍽 Serves: 4

2 sweet potatoes
1 teaspoon salt
½ teaspoon freshly ground black pepper
2 teaspoons olive oil

1. Cut the sweet potatoes lengthwise into ½-inch-thick slices. Then cut each slice into ½-inch-thick fries. 2. In a small mixing bowl, toss the fries with the salt, pepper, and olive oil, making sure that all the potatoes are thoroughly coated with the oil. Add more oil as needed. 3. Insert the crisper plate in the drawer in the lower position, place the sweet potatoes in the drawer, and insert the drawer into the unit. 4. Select AIR FRY, set the temperature to 195°C and set the time to 20 minutes. Select START/STOP to begin cooking. 5. Shake the drawer several times during cooking so that the fries will be evenly cooked and crisp. 6. Remove the drawer, pour the potatoes into a serving bowl, and toss with additional salt and pepper, if desired. Serve and enjoy.

Chapter 2 Vegetables and Sides | 21

Roasted Rosemary Red Potatoes

⏰ Prep Time: 5 minutes   🍲 Cook: 20-22 minutes   🍽 Serves: 4

680g small red potatoes, cut into 1-inch cubes
2 tablespoons olive oil
1 teaspoon salt
½ teaspoon freshly ground black pepper
1 tablespoon minced garlic
2 tablespoons minced fresh rosemary

1. In a medium mixing bowl, combine the diced potatoes, olive oil, pepper, minced garlic, salt, and rosemary and mix well, so the potatoes are thoroughly coated with olive oil. 2. Insert the crisper plate in the drawer in the lower position, place the potatoes in the drawer in a single layer, and insert the drawer into the unit. 3. Select ROAST, set the temperature to 200°C and set the time for 20 minutes. Select START/STOP to begin cooking. Roast for 20 to 22 minutes. 4. Every 5 minutes, remove the and shake, so the potatoes redistribute in the drawer for even cooking. 5. Remove the drawer, pour the potatoes into a large serving bowl, toss with additional salt and pepper. Serve and enjoy.

Cheesy Rice Stuffed Peppers

⏰ Prep Time: 15 minutes   🍲 Cook: 15 minutes   🍽 Serves: 4

4 large red bell peppers
260g cooked rice
40g chopped onion
60g sliced mushrooms
190g marinara sauce
Salt
Pepper
85g shredded mozzarella cheese

1. Boil a large pot of water over high heat. 2. Cut off the tops of the peppers. You can save the tops for decorative plating after you have cooked the peppers. Remove the seeds and hollow out the inside of the peppers. 3. Add the peppers to the boiling water for 5 minutes. Remove and allow them to cool for 3 to 4 minutes. 4. In a large bowl, combine the mushrooms, cooked rice, onion, and marinara sauce. Season with salt and pepper to taste. 5. Stuff the peppers with the rice mixture. Sprinkle the mozzarella cheese on top of the peppers. 6. Insert the crisper plate in the drawer in the lower position, place the stuffed peppers in the drawer, and insert the drawer into the unit. 7. Select ROAST, set the temperature to 175°C and set the time for 10 minutes. Select START/STOP to begin cooking. 8. Cool before serving.

Chinese Vegetable Fried Rice

⏰ Prep Time: 5 minutes   🍲 Cook: 20 minutes   🍽 Serves: 5

2 (255g) packages precooked, microwavable rice
2 teaspoons sesame oil, divided
1 medium green bell pepper, seeded and chopped
150g peas
2 medium carrots, diced (about 110g)
65g chopped onion
Salt
Pepper
1 tablespoon soy sauce
2 medium eggs, scrambled

1. Cook the rice in the microwave according to the package instructions and place in the refrigerator. The rice will need to cool for 15 to 20 minutes. You can also place it in the freezer until cold. 2. Add 1 teaspoon of sesame oil to a pan that fits the air fryer. 3. In a large bowl, combine the cold rice, peas, carrots, green bell pepper, and onion. Drizzle with the remaining 1 teaspoon of sesame oil and stir. Add salt and pepper to taste. 4. Transfer the mixture to the pan. Insert the crisper plate in the drawer in the lower position, place the pan in the drawer, and insert the drawer into the unit. 5. Select AIR FRY, set the temperature to 190°C and set the time to 15 minutes. Select START/STOP to begin cooking. 6. Remove the pan from the drawer. Drizzle the soy sauce all over and add the scrambled eggs. Stir to combine. 7. Serve warm.

Air Fryer Fried Green Tomatoes

⏱ **Prep Time: 15 minutes** 🍳 **Cook: 30 minutes** 🍽 **Serves: 4**

2 green tomatoes
2 eggs
60g all-purpose flour
65g yellow cornmeal
55g panko bread crumbs
1 teaspoon garlic powder
Salt
Pepper
Cooking oil

1. Cut the tomatoes into ½-inch-thick rounds. 2. In a small bowl, beat the eggs. In another small bowl, place the flour. In a third small bowl, combine the yellow cornmeal and panko bread crumbs and season with the garlic powder, salt, and pepper to taste. Mix well to combine. 3. Insert the crisper plate in the drawer in the lower position and spray the crisper plate with the cooking oil. 4. Dip each tomato slice in the flour, then the egg, then the cornmeal, and finally the bread crumb mixture. 5. Working in batches if necessary, place the tomato slices in the drawer. Do not stack. Spray the tomato slices with the cooking oil and insert the drawer into the unit. 6. Select AIR FRY, set the temperature to 200°C and set the time to 5 minutes. Select START/STOP to begin cooking. 7. Remove the drawer and flip the tomatoes. Cook for another 4 to 5 minutes, or until crisp. 8. Remove the cooked tomato slices from the drawer, then repeat to cooking the remaining tomatoes. 9. When done, serve and enjoy.

Baked Sweet Potatoes with Honey Butter

⏱ **Prep Time: 5 minutes** 🍳 **Cook: 40 minutes** 🍽 **Serves: 4**

4 sweet potatoes
2 tablespoons butter
2 tablespoons honey
1 teaspoon cinnamon
½ teaspoon vanilla extract

1. Using a fork, poke three holes in the top of each sweet potato. 2. Insert the crisper plate in the drawer in the lower position, place the sweet potatoes in the drawer, and insert the drawer into the unit. 3. Select BAKE, set the temperature to 200°C and set the time for 40 minutes. Select START/STOP to begin cooking. 4. Meanwhile, in a small, microwave-safe bowl, melt the butter and honey together in the microwave for 15 to 20 seconds. 5. Remove the bowl from the microwave. Add the cinnamon and vanilla extract to the butter and honey mixture, and stir. 6. Remove the cooked sweet potatoes from the drawer and allow them to cool for 5 minutes. 7. Cut open each sweet potato, drizzle the butter mixture over each, and serve.

Air Fried Vegan Chimichanga

⏰ **Prep Time: 2 minutes** 🍲 **Cook: 8 minutes** ❖ **Serves: 1**

1 whole-grain tortilla
120g vegan refried beans
25g grated vegan cheese (optional)
Cooking oil spray (sunflower, safflower, or refined coconut)
130g fresh salsa (or Green Chilli Sauce)
80g chopped romaine lettuce (about ½ head)
Guacamole (optional)
Chopped cilantro (optional)
Cheesy Sauce (optional)

1. Arrange the tortilla on a flat surface and place the beans in the centre. Top with the cheese, if using. Wrap the bottom up over the filling and then fold in the sides. Then roll it all up so as to enclose the beans inside the tortilla (you're making an enclosed burrito here). 2. Insert the crisper plate in the drawer in the lower position and spray the crisper plate with the oil. 3. Place the tortilla wrap inside the drawer, seam-side down, and spray the top of the chimichanga with the oil. 4. Select AIR FRY, set the temperature to 200°C and set the time to 5 minutes. Select START/STOP to begin cooking. 5. Spray the top (and sides) again with the oil, flip over, and spray the other side with the oil. Air fry for an additional 2 or 3 minutes, until nicely browned and crisp. 6. Transfer to a plate. Top with the salsa, lettuce, guacamole, cilantro, and/or Cheesy Sauce, if using. Serve immediately.

Cheesy Refried Bean Taquitos

⏰ **Prep Time: 5 minutes** 🍲 **Cook: 7 minutes** ❖ **Serves: 4**

8 corn tortillas
Cooking oil spray (coconut, sunflower, or safflower)
1 (425g) can vegan refried beans
100g shredded vegan cheese
Guacamole (optional)
Cheesy Sauce (optional)
Vegan sour cream (optional)
Fresh salsa (optional)

1. Insert the crisper plate in the drawer in the lower position and spray the crisper plate with the cooking oil spray. 2. Warm the tortillas (so they don't break): Run them under water for a second and then place in an oil-sprayed air fryer drawer (stacking them is fine). Insert the drawer into the unit. 3. Select AIR FRY, set the temperature to 200°C and set the time to 1 minute. Select START/STOP to begin cooking. 4. Remove the tortillas to a flat surface, laying them out individually. Place an equal amount of the beans in a line down the centre of each tortilla. Top with the vegan cheese. 5. Roll the tortilla sides up over the filling and place seam-side down in the drawer (this will help them seal so the tortillas don't fly open). Add just enough to fill the drawer without them touching too much (you may need to do another batch, depending on the size of your air fryer drawer). 6. Spray the tops with the oil and air fry for 7 minutes, or until the tortillas are golden-brown and lightly crisp. 7. Serve immediately with your preferred toppings.

Chapter 2 Vegetables and Sides

Tomato and Spinach Stuffed Portobello Mushrooms

⏱ **Prep Time: 10 minutes** 🍴 **Cook: 10-12 minutes** 🍽 **Serves: 4**

4 large Portobello mushroom caps (about 85g each)
Olive oil spray
Kosher salt
2 medium plum tomatoes, chopped
30g baby spinach, roughly chopped
40g crumbled feta cheese
1 shallot, chopped
1 large garlic clove, minced
5g chopped fresh basil
2 tablespoons panko bread crumbs, regular or gluten-free
1 tablespoon chopped fresh oregano
1 tablespoon freshly grated Parmesan cheese
⅛ teaspoon freshly ground black pepper
1 tablespoon olive oil
Balsamic glaze (optional), for drizzling

1. Use a small metal spoon to carefully scrape the black gills out of each mushroom cap. Spray both sides of the mushrooms with the olive oil and season with a pinch of salt. 2. In a medium bowl, combine the tomatoes, shallot, spinach, garlic, feta, basil, panko, Parmesan, ¼ teaspoon salt, oregano, pepper, and olive oil and mix well. Carefully fill the inside of each mushroom cap with the mixture. 3. Insert the crisper plate in the drawer in the lower position. Working in batches, arrange a single layer of the stuffed mushrooms in the drawer and insert the drawer into the unit. 4. Select ROAST, set the temperature to 185°C and set the time for 10 minutes. Select START/STOP to begin cooking. Cook for 10 to 12 minutes, until the mushrooms are tender and the top is golden. 5. Use a flexible spatula to carefully remove the mushrooms from the drawer and transfer to a serving dish. Drizzle the balsamic glaze (if using) over the mushrooms and serve.

Sesame Crusted Tofu Steaks

⏱ **Prep Time: 10 minutes** 🍴 **Cook: 10 minutes** 🍽 **Serves: 2**

Sriracha Mayo:
4 teaspoons mayonnaise
1 teaspoon Sriracha sauce

Tofu:
200g extra-firm tofu (about ½ block), drained and cut into 4 (½-inch-thick) slices
2 tablespoons reduced-sodium soy sauce or tamari
1 teaspoon toasted sesame oil
1 teaspoon unseasoned rice vinegar
1 teaspoon light brown sugar
1 garlic clove, grated
½ teaspoon grated fresh ginger
40g white and black sesame seeds
1 large egg
Olive oil spray
1 scallion, chopped, for garnish (optional)

For the Sriracha mayo: 1. In a small bowl, combine the mayonnaise and Sriracha.
For the tofu: 1. Arrange the tofu slices on a kitchen towel or paper towels. Place another towel on top and press gently to remove most of the water from the tofu. Transfer to a shallow bowl or baking dish that is big enough to spread the tofu into a single layer. 2. In a small bowl, whisk together the vinegar, brown sugar, soy sauce, garlic, sesame oil, and ginger. Drizzle half of the marinade over the tofu, then gently flip, and drizzle the rest over the other side. Marinate in the refrigerator for at least 1 hour, or up to overnight. 3. Put the sesame seeds on a small plate or pie dish. In another small dish or bowl, beat the egg. 4. Remove each tofu slice from the marinade, letting the excess drip off, and then dip in the egg. 5. Using a fork, dip in the sesame seeds, coating each side. Transfer to a work surface. Spray one side with the olive oil, then gently flip, and spray the other side. (Discard the excess marinade.) 6. Insert the crisper plate in the drawer in the lower position. Working in batches, place a single layer of the tofu in the drawer and insert the drawer into the unit. 7. Select AIR FRY, set the temperature to 200°C and set the time for 10 minutes. Select START/STOP to begin cooking. Cook, flipping halfway, until toasted and crisp. 8. To serve, top each tofu "steak" with the Sriracha mayo and some scallion (if using).

Chapter 2 Vegetables and Sides

Air-Fried Cheese Sandwich

⏰ Prep Time: 3 minutes　🍲 Cook: 12 minutes　🍽 Serves: 1

2 slices sprouted whole-grain bread (or substitute a gluten-free bread)
1 teaspoon vegan margarine or neutral-flavoured oil (sunflower, safflower, or refined coconut)
2 slices vegan cheese (Violife cheddar or Chao creamy original) or Cheesy Sauce
1 teaspoon mellow white miso
1 medium-large garlic clove, pressed or finely minced
2 tablespoons fermented vegetables, kimchi, or sauerkraut
Romaine or green leaf lettuce

1. Spread the outsides of the bread with the vegan margarine. Place the sliced cheese inside and close the sandwich back up again (buttered sides facing out). 2. Insert the crisper plate in the drawer in the lower position, place the sandwich in the drawer, and insert the drawer into the unit. Select AIR FRY, set the temperature to 200°C and set the time to 6 minutes. Select START/STOP to begin cooking. 3. Flip over and fry for another 6 minutes, or until nicely browned and crisp on the outside. 4. Transfer to a plate. Open the sandwich and evenly spread the miso and garlic clove over the inside of one of the bread slices. Top with the fermented vegetables and lettuce, close the sandwich back up, cut in half, and serve immediately.

Tamale Pie with Cornmeal Crust

⏰ Prep Time: 25 minutes　🍲 Cook: 20 minutes　🍽 Serves: 4

For the Filling:
1 medium courgette, diced
2 teaspoons neutral-flavoured oil (sunflower, safflower, or refined coconut)
170g cooked pinto beans, drained
240g canned diced tomatoes (unsalted) with juice
3 large garlic cloves, minced or pressed
1 tablespoon chickpea flour
1 teaspoon dried oregano
1 teaspoon onion granules
½ teaspoon salt
½ teaspoon crushed red chilli flakes
Cooking oil spray (sunflower, safflower, or refined coconut)

For the Crust:
65g yellow cornmeal, finely ground
360ml water
½ teaspoon salt
1 teaspoon nutritional yeast
1 teaspoon neutral-flavoured oil (sunflower, safflower, or refined coconut)
2 tablespoons finely chopped coriander
½ teaspoon lime zest

To make the filling: 1. In a large skillet set to medium-high heat, sauté the courgette and oil for 3 minutes, or until the courgette begins to brown. 2. Add the beans, flour, oregano, tomatoes, garlic, onion, salt, and chilli flakes to the mixture. Cook over medium heat, stirring often, for 5 minutes, or until the mixture is thickened and no liquid remains. Remove from the heat. 3. Spray a baking pan that fits your air fryer with oil and place the mixture in the bottom. Smooth out the top and set aside.
To make the crust: 1. In a medium pot over high heat, place the cornmeal, water, and salt. Whisk constantly as you bring the mixture to a boil. Once it boils, reduce the heat to very low. Add the nutritional yeast and oil and continue to cook, stirring very often, for 10 minutes or until the mixture is very thick and hard to whisk. Remove from the heat. 2. Stir the coriander and lime zest into the cornmeal mixture until thoroughly combined. Using a rubber spatula, gently spread it evenly onto the filling in the baking pan to form a smooth crust topping. 3. Place the pan in the drawer and insert the drawer into the unit. Select BAKE, set the temperature to 160°C and set the time for 20 minutes. Select START/STOP to begin cooking. Bake until the top is golden-brown. 4. Let it cool for 5 to 10 minutes, then cut and serve.

Chapter 3 Snacks and Starters

28 Air Fried Cheddar Sandwich
28 Homemade Mozzarella Cheese Sticks
28 Crispy Potato Chips
29 Crispy Jalapeño Poppers
29 Loaded Baked Potato Skins
30 Crispy Kale Chips
30 Bacon Wrapped Jalapeño Poppers
30 Crispy Sweet Potato Chips
31 Parmesan Dill Fried Pickles
31 Parmesan Courgette Chips with Lemon Aioli
32 Cinnamon Spiced Nuts
32 Jalapeño Cheese Balls
33 Greek Street Taco Hand Pies
33 Air Fried Stuffed Mushrooms

Air Fried Cheddar Sandwich

⏰ Prep Time: 5 minutes   🍲 Cook: 5 minutes   ⬥ Serves: 2

4 slices bread
115g Cheddar cheese slices
2 teaspoons butter or oil

1. Lay the four cheese slices on two of the bread slices and top with the remaining two slices of bread. 2. Brush both sides with butter or oil and cut the sandwiches in rectangular halves. 3. Insert the crisper plate in the drawer in the lower position, place the sandwiches in the drawer, and insert the drawer into the unit. 4. Select AIR FRY, set the temperature to 200°C and set the time to 5 minutes. Select START/STOP to begin cooking. Cook until the outside is crisp and the cheese melts. 5. When done, serve and enjoy.

Homemade Mozzarella Cheese Sticks

⏰ Prep Time: 10 minutes   🍲 Cook: 14 minutes   ⬥ Serves: 4

1 egg
1 tablespoon water
8 eggroll wraps
8 mozzarella string cheese "sticks"
Sauce for dipping

1. Beat together the egg and water in a small bowl. 2. Lay out the eggroll wraps and moisten edges with the egg wash. 3. Place one piece of string cheese on each wrap near one end. 4. Fold in sides of eggroll wrap over ends of cheese and then roll up. 5. Brush outside of wrap with the egg wash and press gently to seal well. 6. Insert the crisper plate in the drawer in the lower position. Place the wraps in the drawer in a single layer. Insert the drawer into the unit. 7. Select AIR FRY, set the temperature to 200°C and set the time to 5 minutes. Select START/STOP to begin cooking. 8. Cook an additional 1 or 2 minutes, if necessary, until they are golden brown and crispy. 9. Serve with your favourite dipping sauce.

Crispy Potato Chips

⏰ Prep Time: 5 minutes   🍲 Cook: 15-25 minutes   ⬥ Serves: 4

4 yellow potatoes
1 tablespoon olive oil
1 tablespoon salt (plus more for topping)

1. Using a sharp knife or mandoline, slice the potatoes into ⅛-inch-thick slices. 2. In a medium mixing bowl, toss the potato slices with the olive oil and salt until the potato slices are thoroughly coated with the oil. 3. Insert the crisper plate in the drawer in the lower position. Place the potatoes in the drawer in a single layer. (You may have to fry the potato chips in more than one batch.) Insert the drawer into the unit. 4. Select AIR FRY, set the temperature to 190°C and set the time to 15 minutes. Select START/STOP to begin cooking. 5. Shake the drawer several times during cooking, so the chips crisp evenly and don't burn. 6. Check to see if they are fork-tender; if not, add another 5 to 10 minutes, checking frequently. They will crisp up after they are removed from the drawer. 7. Season with additional salt, if desired.

| Chapter 3 Snacks and Starters

Crispy Jalapeño Poppers

⏰ Prep Time: 60 minutes　🍳 Cook: 5 minutes　🍽 Serves: 4

225g jalapeño peppers
30g cornstarch
1 egg
1 tablespoon lime juice
30g plain breadcrumbs
30g panko breadcrumbs
½ teaspoon salt
Oil for misting or cooking spray

Filling:
115g cream cheese
1 teaspoon grated lime zest
¼ teaspoon chilli powder
⅛ teaspoon garlic powder
¼ teaspoon salt

1. Combine all filling ingredients in a small bowl and mix well. Refrigerate while preparing peppers. 2. Cut the jalapeños into ½-inch lengthwise slices. Use a small, sharp knife to remove the seeds and veins. If you want the mild appetisers, discard seeds and veins; or if you want the hot appetisers, finely chop seeds and veins. Stir a small amount into filling, taste, and continue adding a little at a time until filling is as hot as you like. 3. Stuff each pepper slice with the filling. 4. Place the cornstarch in a shallow dish. 5. In another shallow dish, beat together the egg and lime juice. 6. Place the breadcrumbs and salt in a third shallow dish and stir together. 7. Dip each pepper slice in the cornstarch, shake off excess, and dip in the egg mixture. 8. Roll in the breadcrumbs, pressing to make the coating stick. 9. Place the pepper slices on a plate in single layer and freeze them for 30 minutes. 10. Insert the crisper plate in the drawer in the lower position. Spray the frozen peppers with the oil or cooking spray and place in the drawer in a single layer. Insert the drawer into the unit. 11. Select AIR FRY, set the temperature to 200°C and set the time to 5 minutes. Select START/STOP to begin cooking. 12. When done, serve and enjoy.

Loaded Baked Potato Skins

⏰ Prep Time: 10 minutes　🍳 Cook: 12 minutes　🍽 Serves: 4

4 medium russet potatoes, baked
Olive oil
Salt
Freshly ground black pepper
225g shredded Cheddar cheese
4 slices cooked bacon, chopped
Finely chopped scallions, for topping
Sour cream, for topping
Finely chopped olives, for topping

1. Insert the crisper plate in the drawer in the lower position and spray the crisper plate with the oil. 2. Cut each baked potato in half. 3. Using a large spoon, scoop out the centre of each potato half, leaving about 1 inch of the potato flesh around the edges and the bottom. 4. Rub the olive oil over the inside of each baked potato half and season with the salt and pepper, then place the potato skins in the greased drawer. Insert the drawer into the unit. 5. Select BAKE, set the temperature to 200°C and set the time for 10 minutes. Select START/STOP to begin cooking. 6. After 10 minutes, remove the potato skins and fill them with the shredded Cheddar cheese and bacon. Continue to bake in the air fryer for another 2 minutes, just until the cheese is melted. 7. Garnish the potato skins with the scallions, sour cream, and olives.

Chapter 3 Snacks and Starters | 29

Crispy Kale Chips

⏰ Prep Time: 5 minutes 🍲 Cook: 10 minutes ❖ Serves: 4

1 bunch fresh kale, ribs removed, chopped into large pieces
1 tablespoon extra-virgin olive oil
Salt
Pepper

1. In a large bowl, combine the kale and olive oil and season with the salt and pepper. Mix well to ensure the kale is fully coated. 2. Insert the crisper plate in the drawer in the lower position, place the kale in the drawer, and insert the drawer into the unit. 3. Select AIR FRY, set the temperature to 135°C and set the time to 5 minutes. Select START/STOP to begin cooking. 4. Remove the drawer, shake, and continue to cook for an additional 5 minutes. 5. Cool before serving.

Bacon Wrapped Jalapeño Poppers

⏰ Prep Time: 5 minutes 🍲 Cook: 12 minutes ❖ Serves: 12

12 jalapeño peppers
1 (230g) package cream cheese, at room temperature
115g shredded Cheddar cheese
1 teaspoon onion powder
1 teaspoon salt
½ teaspoon freshly ground black pepper
12 slices bacon, cut in half

1. Insert the crisper plate in the drawer in the lower position and spray the crisper plate with the olive oil. 2. Cut each pepper in half, then use a spoon to scrape out the veins and seeds. 3. In a small mixing bowl, mix together the cream cheese, onion powder, salt, Cheddar cheese, and pepper. 4. Using a small spoon, fill each pepper half with the cheese mixture. 5. Wrap each stuffed pepper half with a half slice of bacon. 6. Place the bacon-wrapped peppers into the greased drawer in a single layer. (You may have to cook the peppers in more than one batch.) Insert the drawer into the unit. 7. Select BAKE, set the temperature to 160°C and set the time for 12 minutes. Select START/STOP to begin cooking. 8. Using tongs, remove the peppers from the drawer, place them on a platter, and serve.

Crispy Sweet Potato Chips

⏰ Prep Time: 10 minutes 🍲 Cook: 20 minutes ❖ Serves: 5

3 sweet potatoes
2 teaspoons extra-virgin olive oil
1 teaspoon cinnamon (optional)
Salt
Pepper

1. Peel the sweet potatoes using a vegetable peeler. Cut the potatoes crosswise into thin slices. You can also use a mandoline to slice the potatoes into chips. 2. Put the sweet potatoes in a large bowl of cold water for 30 minutes. This helps remove the starch from the sweet potatoes, which promotes crisping. 3. Drain the sweet potatoes. Dry the sweet potato slices thoroughly with paper towels or napkins. 4. Place the sweet potatoes in another large bowl. Drizzle with the olive oil and sprinkle with the cinnamon (if using), salt, and pepper to taste. Toss to fully coat. 5. Place the sweet potato slices in the drawer. It is okay to stack them, but do not overcrowd. You may need to cook the chips in two batches. Insert the drawer into the unit. 6. Select AIR FRY, set the temperature to 200°C and set the time to 10 minutes. Select START/STOP to begin cooking. 7. Remove the drawer and shake. Continue to cook the chips for an additional 10 minutes. 8. Cool before serving.

Parmesan Dill Fried Pickles

⏰ Prep Time: 5 minutes   🍲 Cook: 4 minutes   📚 Serves: 4

1 (450g) jar sliced dill pickles
35g panko bread crumbs
35g grated Parmesan cheese
¼ teaspoon dried dill
2 large eggs

1. Line a platter with a double thickness of paper towels. Spread the pickles out in a single layer on the paper towels. Let the pickles drain on the towels for 20 minutes. After 20 minutes have passed, pat the pickles again with a clean paper towel to get them as dry as possible before breading. 2. Insert the crisper plate in the drawer in the lower position and spray the crisper plate with the olive oil. 3. In a small mixing bowl, combine the panko bread crumbs, Parmesan cheese, and dried dill. Mix well. 4. In a separate small bowl, crack the eggs and beat until frothy. 5. Dip each pickle into the egg mixture, then into the bread crumb mixture. Make sure the pickle is fully coated in breading. 6. Place the breaded pickle slices in the greased drawer in a single layer. (You may have to fry your pickles in more than one batch.) Insert the drawer into the unit. 7. Spray the pickles with a generous amount of olive oil. 8. Select AIR FRY, set the temperature to 200°C and set the time to 4 minutes. Select START/STOP to begin cooking. 9. Remove the drawer and use tongs to flip the pickles. Spray them again with the olive oil and continue to air fry for another 4 minutes. 10. Using tongs, remove the pickles from the drawer. Plate, serve, and enjoy!

Parmesan Courgette Chips with Lemon Aioli

⏰ Prep Time: 15 minutes   🍲 Cook: 20 minutes   📚 Serves: 5

For the Courgette Chips:
2 medium courgette
2 eggs
35g bread crumbs
35g grated Parmesan cheese
Salt
Pepper
Cooking oil

For the Lemon Aioli:
110g mayonnaise
½ tablespoon olive oil
Juice of ½ lemon
1 teaspoon minced garlic
Salt
Pepper

To make the courgette chips: 1. Slice the courgette into thin chips, about ⅛ inch thick with a knife or mandoline. 2. In a small bowl, beat the eggs. In another small bowl, combine the bread crumbs, Parmesan cheese, salt, and pepper. 3. Insert the crisper plate in the drawer in the lower position and spray the crisper plate with the cooking oil. 4. Dip the courgette slices one at a time in the eggs and then the bread crumb mixture. You can also sprinkle the bread crumbs onto the courgette slices with a spoon. 5. Working in batches, place the courgette chips in the drawer, but do not stack. Spray the chips with the cooking oil from a distance (otherwise, the breading may fly off), and insert the drawer into the unit. 6. Select AIR FRY, set the temperature to 175°C and set the time to 10 minutes. Select START/STOP to begin cooking. 7. Remove the cooked courgette chips from the drawer, then repeat to cook the remaining courgette.
To make the lemon aioli: 1. While the courgette is cooking, combine the mayonnaise, olive oil, lemon juice, and garlic in a small bowl, adding salt and pepper to taste. Mix well until fully combined. 2. Cool the courgette chips and serve alongside the aioli.

Chapter 3 Snacks and Starters | 31

Cinnamon Spiced Nuts

⏰ **Prep Time: 5 minutes**　🍲 **Cook: 15 minutes**　🍃 **Serves: 4**

½ teaspoon cinnamon
½ teaspoon stevia
Pepper
120g nuts (walnuts, pecans, and almonds work well)
1 egg white
Cooking oil

1. In a small bowl, combine the cinnamon, stevia, and pepper to taste. 2. Place the nuts in another bowl with the egg white. Add the spices to the nuts. 3. Insert the crisper plate in the drawer in the lower position and spray the crisper plate with the cooking oil. 4. Place the nuts in the drawer. Spray them with cooking oil and insert the drawer into the unit. 5. Select ROAST, set the temperature to 150°C and set the time for 10 minutes. Select START/STOP to begin cooking. 6. Remove the drawer, shake and continue to cook for an additional 3 to 4 minutes. 7. Serve warm.

Jalapeño Cheese Balls

⏰ **Prep Time: 15 minutes**　🍲 **Cook: 15 minutes**　🍃 **Serves: 12**

115g cream cheese
40g shredded mozzarella cheese
35g shredded Cheddar cheese
2 jalapeños, finely chopped
55g bread crumbs
2 eggs
60g all-purpose flour
Salt
Pepper
Cooking oil

1. In a medium bowl, combine the cream cheese, mozzarella, Cheddar, and jalapeños. Mix well. 2. Form the cheese mixture into balls about an inch thick. Using a small ice cream scoop works well. 3. Arrange the cheese balls on a sheet pan and place in the freezer for 15 minutes. This will help the cheese balls maintain their shape while frying. 4. Insert the crisper plate in the drawer in the lower position and spray the crisper plate with the cooking oil. 5. Add the bread crumbs in a small bowl. In another small bowl, beat the eggs. In a third small bowl, combine the flour with the salt and pepper to taste, and mix well. 6. Remove the cheese balls from the freezer. Dip the cheese balls in the flour, then the eggs, and then the bread crumbs. 7. Place the cheese balls in the drawer. (It is okay to stack them.) Spray with the cooking oil and insert the drawer into the unit. 8. Select AIR FRY, set the temperature to 200°C and set the time to 8 minutes. Select START/STOP to begin cooking. 9. Remove the drawer and flip the cheese balls. I recommend flipping them instead of shaking so the balls maintain their form. Continue to cook an additional 4 minutes. 10. Cool before serving.

Greek Street Taco Hand Pies

⏱ **Prep Time: 10 minutes** 🍳 **Cook: 3 minutes** ◆ **Serves: 4**

8 small flour tortillas (4-inch diameter)
8 tablespoons hummus
4 tablespoons crumbled feta cheese
4 tablespoons chopped Kalamata or other olives (optional)
Olive oil for misting

1. Place 1 tablespoon of hummus or tapenade in the centre of each tortilla. Top with 1 teaspoon of feta crumbles and 1 teaspoon of chopped olives, if using. 2. Using your finger or a small spoon, moisten the edges of the tortilla all around with water. 3. Fold tortilla over to make a half-moon shape. Press centre gently. Then press the edges firmly to seal in the filling. 4. Mist both sides with olive oil. 5. Insert the crisper plate in the drawer in the lower position, place the pies in the drawer very close but try not to overlap, and insert the drawer into the unit. Select AIR FRY, set the temperature to 200°C and set the time to 3 minutes. Select START/STOP to begin cooking. Cook just until lightly browned and crispy. 6. When done, serve and enjoy.

Air Fried Stuffed Mushrooms

⏱ **Prep Time: 5 minutes** 🍳 **Cook: 10 minutes** ◆ **Serves: 4**

12 medium button mushrooms
55g bread crumbs
1 teaspoon salt
½ teaspoon freshly ground black pepper
5 to 6 tablespoons olive oil

1. Insert the crisper plate in the drawer in the lower position and spray the crisper plate with the olive oil. 2. Separate the cap from the stem of each mushroom. Discard the stems. 3. In a small mixing bowl, combine the salt, bread crumbs, pepper, and olive oil until you have a wet mixture. 4. Rub the mushrooms with the olive oil on all sides. 5. Using a spoon, fill each mushroom with the bread crumb stuffing. 6. Place the mushrooms in the greased drawer in a single layer and insert the drawer into the unit. Select BAKE, set the temperature to 180°C and set the time to 10 minutes. Select START/STOP to begin cooking. 7. Using tongs, remove the mushrooms from the air fryer, place them on a platter, and serve.

Chapter 3 Snacks and Starters

Chapter 4 Poultry

- 35 Authentic Chicken Parmesan
- 35 Air Fryer Jerk Chicken Thighs
- 36 Delicious Tandoori Chicken Thighs
- 36 Crispy Pickle-Brined Fried Chicken
- 37 Feta and Spinach Stuffed Chicken Breasts
- 37 Brazilian Tempero Baiano Chicken Drumsticks
- 38 Greek Turkey Burgers with Tzatziki Sauce
- 38 Spinach and Feta Chicken Meatballs
- 39 Garlic Chicken Wings with Green Beans and Rice
- 39 Spicy Black Bean Turkey Burgers with Avocado Spread
- 40 Classic Nashville Hot Chicken
- 40 Maple Bacon Wrapped Chicken Breasts
- 41 Thai Courgette Turkey Meatballs
- 41 Teriyaki Chicken Drumsticks
- 42 Garlic Butter Chicken
- 42 Marinated Ginger Chicken

Authentic Chicken Parmesan

⏱ **Prep Time: 10 minutes** 🍱 **Cook: 18-20 minutes** 🍽 **Serves: 4**

2 large skinless chicken breasts (about 570g)
Salt and freshly ground black pepper
55g almond meal
50g grated Parmesan cheese
2 teaspoons Italian seasoning
1 egg, lightly beaten
1 tablespoon olive oil
250g no-sugar-added marinara sauce
4 slices mozzarella cheese or 55g shredded mozzarella

1. Slice the chicken breasts in half horizontally to create 4 thinner chicken breasts. Working with one piece at a time, place the chicken between two pieces of parchment paper and pound with a rolling pin or meat mallet to flatten to an even thickness. Season both sides with the salt and freshly ground black pepper. 2. In a large shallow bowl, combine the almond meal, Parmesan, and Italian seasoning and stir until thoroughly combined. Place the egg in another large shallow bowl. 3. Dip the chicken in the egg, followed by the almond meal mixture, pressing the mixture firmly into the chicken to create an even coating. 4. Insert the crisper plate in the drawer in the lower position. Working in batches if necessary, arrange the chicken breasts in a single layer in the drawer and coat both sides lightly with the vegetable oil. Insert the drawer into the unit. 5. Select AIR FRY, set the temperature to 180°C and set the time to 15 minutes. Select START/STOP to begin cooking. 6. Cook until a thermometer inserted into the thickest part registers 75°C, pausing halfway through the cooking time to flip the chicken. 7. Spoon the marinara sauce over each piece of chicken and top with the mozzarella cheese. Continue to air fry for an additional 3 to 5 minutes until the cheese is melted. 8. When done, serve and enjoy.

Air Fryer Jerk Chicken Thighs

⏱ **Prep Time: 10 minutes** 🍱 **Cook: 15-20 minutes** 🍽 **Serves: 6**

2 teaspoons ground coriander
1 teaspoon ground allspice
1 teaspoon cayenne pepper
1 teaspoon ground ginger
1 teaspoon salt
1 teaspoon dried thyme
½ teaspoon ground cinnamon
½ teaspoon ground nutmeg
910g boneless chicken thighs, skin on
2 tablespoons vegetable oil

1. In a small bowl, combine the allspice, coriander, ginger, salt, thyme, cayenne, cinnamon, and nutmeg. Stir until thoroughly combined. 2. Place the chicken in a baking dish and use paper towels to pat dry. Thoroughly coat both sides of the chicken with the spice mixture. Cover and refrigerate for at least 2 hours, preferably overnight. 3. Insert the crisper plate in the drawer in the lower position. Working in batches if necessary, place the chicken in a single layer in the drawer and coat lightly with the vegetable oil. Insert the drawer into the unit. 4. Select AIR FRY, set the temperature to 180°C and set the time to 15 minutes. Select START/STOP to begin cooking. 5. Cook for 15 to 20 minutes until a thermometer inserted into the thickest part registers 75°C, pausing halfway through the cooking time to flip the chicken. 6. When done, serve and enjoy.

Delicious Tandoori Chicken Thighs

⏲ Prep Time: 10 minutes　🍳 Cook: 15-20 minutes　🍽 Serves: 6

80g plain Greek yoghurt
2 cloves garlic, minced
1 tablespoon grated fresh ginger
½ teaspoon ground cayenne
½ teaspoon ground turmeric
½ teaspoon garam masala
1 teaspoon ground cumin
1 teaspoon salt
910g boneless chicken thighs, skin on
2 tablespoons chopped fresh cilantro
1 lemon, cut into 6 wedges
½ sweet onion, sliced

1. In a small bowl, combine the yoghurt, garlic, turmeric, garam masala, ginger, cayenne, cumin, and salt. Whisk until thoroughly combined. 2. Transfer the yoghurt mixture to a large resealable bag. Add the chicken, seal the bag, and massage the bag to ensure chicken is evenly coated. Refrigerate for 1 hour (or up to 8 hours). 3. Insert the crisper plate in the drawer in the lower position. Remove the chicken from the marinade, discard the marinade, and arrange in a single layer in the drawer. Insert the drawer into the unit. 4. Select AIR FRY, set the temperature to 180°C and set the time to 15 minutes. Select START/STOP to begin cooking. Cook for 15 to 20 minutes until a thermometer inserted into the thickest part registers 75°C, pausing halfway through the cooking time to flip the chicken. 5. Transfer the chicken to a serving platter, top with the cilantro, and serve with the lemon wedges and sliced onion.

Crispy Pickle-Brined Fried Chicken

⏲ Prep Time: 7 minutes　🍳 Cook: 20 minutes　🍽 Serves: 4

4 bone-in, skin-on chicken legs, cut into drumsticks and thighs (about 1595g)
Pickle juice from a 680g jar of kosher dill pickles
55g flour
Salt and freshly ground black pepper
2 eggs
110g fine breadcrumbs
1 teaspoon salt
1 teaspoon freshly ground black pepper
½ teaspoon ground paprika
⅛ teaspoon ground cayenne pepper
Vegetable or canola oil in a spray bottle

1. Put the chicken in a shallow dish and pour the pickle juice over. Cover and place the chicken in the refrigerator to brine in the pickle juice for 3 to 8 hours. 2. When ready to cook, remove the chicken from the refrigerator and let come to room temperature while setting up a dredging station. Place the flour in a shallow dish and season well with the salt and freshly ground black pepper. Whisk the eggs in a second shallow dish. In a third shallow dish, combine the breadcrumbs, paprika, pepper, salt, and cayenne pepper. 3. Remove the chicken from the pickle brine and gently pat dry with a clean kitchen towel. Dredge each piece of chicken in the flour, then dip into the egg mixture, and finally press into the breadcrumb mixture to coat all sides of the chicken. Arrange the breaded chicken on a baking sheet or plate and spray each piece all over with the vegetable oil. 4. Insert the crisper plate in the drawer in the lower position. Air fry the chicken in two batches. Place two chicken thighs and two drumsticks in the drawer and insert the drawer into the unit. 5. Select AIR FRY, set the temperature to 185°C and set the time to 10 minutes. Select START/STOP to begin cooking. 6. Then, gently turn the chicken pieces over and air-fry for another 10 minutes. 7. Remove the chicken pieces and let them rest on plate – do not cover. Repeat with the second batch of chicken, air-frying for 20 minutes, turning the chicken over halfway through. 8. Lower the temperature of the air fryer to 170°C. Place the first batch of chicken on top of the second batch already in the drawer and air-fry for another 7 minutes. 9. Serve warm and enjoy.

Feta and Spinach Stuffed Chicken Breasts

⏰ **Prep Time: 3 minutes** 🍲 **Cook: 12 minutes** 🍽 **Serves: 4**

1 (285g) package frozen spinach, thawed and drained well
110g feta cheese, crumbled
½ teaspoon freshly ground black pepper
4 boneless chicken breasts
Salt and freshly ground black pepper
1 tablespoon olive oil

1. Prepare the filling. Squeeze out as much liquid as possible from the thawed spinach. Rough chop the spinach and transfer to a mixing bowl with the feta cheese and the freshly ground black pepper. 2. Prepare the chicken breast. Arrange the chicken breast on a cutting board and press down on the chicken breast with one hand to keep it stabilised. Make an incision about 1-inch long in the fattest side of the breast. Move the knife up and down inside the chicken breast, without poking through either the top or the bottom, or the other side of the breast. The inside pocket should be about 3-inches long, but the opening should only be about 1-inch wide. If this is too difficult, you can make the incision longer, but you will have to be more careful when cooking the chicken breast since this will expose more of the stuffing. 3. Once you have prepared the chicken breasts, use your fingers to stuff the filling into each pocket, spreading the mixture down as far as you can. 4. Insert the crisper plate in the drawer in the lower position. Lightly brush or spray the crisper plate and the chicken breasts with the olive oil. Transfer two of the stuffed chicken breasts to the drawer and insert the drawer into the unit. 5. Select AIR FRY, set the temperature to 195°C and set the time to 12 minutes. Select START/STOP to begin cooking. 6. Turn the chicken breasts over halfway through the cooking time. 7. Remove the chicken to a resting plate and air-fry the second two breasts for 12 minutes. 8. Return the first batch of chicken to the drawer with the second batch and air-fry for 3 more minutes. 9. When the chicken is cooked, an instant read thermometer should register 75°C in the thickest part of the chicken, as well as in the stuffing. 10. Remove the chicken breasts from air fryer and let rest on a cutting board for 2 to 3 minutes. Slice the chicken on the bias and serve with the slices fanned out.

Brazilian Tempero Baiano Chicken Drumsticks

⏰ **Prep Time: 5 minutes** 🍲 **Cook: 20 minutes** 🍽 **Serves: 4**

1 teaspoon cumin seeds
1 teaspoon dried oregano
1 teaspoon dried parsley
1 teaspoon ground turmeric
½ teaspoon coriander seeds
1 teaspoon kosher salt
½ teaspoon black peppercorns
½ teaspoon cayenne pepper
60ml fresh lime juice
2 tablespoons olive oil
680g chicken drumsticks

1. In a clean coffee grinder or spice mill, combine the cumin, oregano, coriander seeds, salt, parsley, turmeric, peppercorns, and cayenne. Process until finely ground. 2. In a small bowl, combine the ground spices with the lime juice and oil. Place the chicken in a resealable plastic bag. Add the marinade, seal, and massage until the chicken is well coated. Marinate at room temperature for 30 minutes or in the refrigerator for up to 24 hours. 3. Insert the crisper plate in the drawer in the lower position, place the drumsticks skin side up in the drawer, and insert the drawer into the unit. 4. Select AIR FRY, set the temperature to 200°C and set the time to 20 minutes. Select START/STOP to begin cooking. Cook for 20 to 25 minutes, turning the legs halfway through the cooking time. Use a meat thermometer to ensure that the chicken has reached an internal temperature of 75°C. 5. Serve and enjoy.

Greek Turkey Burgers with Tzatziki Sauce

⏰ **Prep Time:** 25 minutes   🍲 **Cook:** 12 minutes   ❖ **Serves:** 4

For the Tzatziki:
1 large cucumber, peeled and grated (about 240g)
2 to 3 cloves garlic, minced
245g plain Greek yoghurt
1 tablespoon tahini (sesame paste)
1 tablespoon fresh lemon juice
½ teaspoon kosher salt

For the Burgers:
455g ground turkey, chicken, or lamb
1 small yellow onion, finely diced
1 clove garlic, minced
2 tablespoons chopped fresh parsley
2 teaspoons Lebanese Seven-Spice Mix
½ teaspoon kosher salt
Vegetable oil spray

For Serving:
4 lettuce leaves or 2 whole-wheat pita breads, halved
8 slices ripe tomato
30g baby spinach
35g crumbled feta cheese

For the tzatziki: 1. In a medium bowl, stir together all the ingredients until well combined. Cover and chill until ready to serve.
For the burgers: 1. In a large bowl, combine the ground turkey, parsley, spice mix, onion, garlic, and salt. Mix gently until well combined. Divide the turkey into four portions and form into round patties. 2. Insert the crisper plate in the drawer in the lower position and spray the crisper plate with the vegetable oil spray. Place the patties in a single layer in the drawer and insert the drawer into the unit. 3. Select ROAST, set the temperature to 200°C and set the time for 12 minutes. Select START/STOP to begin cooking. 4. Use a meat thermometer to ensure the burgers have reached an internal temperature of 75°C (for turkey or chicken) or 70°C (for lamb).
For serving: 1. Place one burger in each lettuce leaf or pita half. Tuck in 2 tomato slices, spinach, cheese, and some tzatziki. Serve and enjoy.

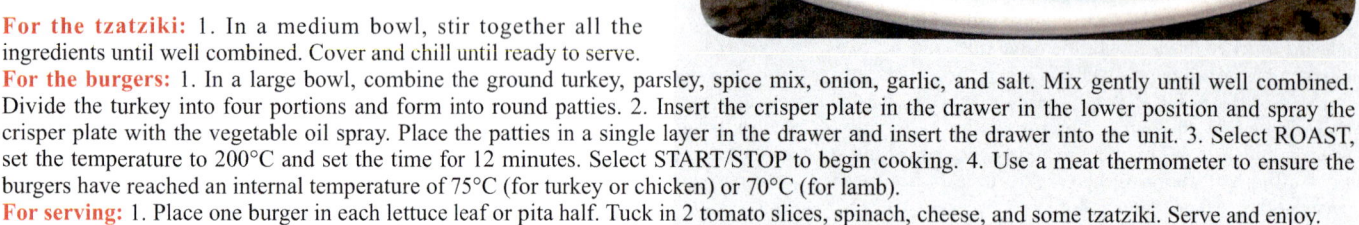

Spinach and Feta Chicken Meatballs

⏰ **Prep Time:** 10 minutes   🍲 **Cook:** 12 minutes   ❖ **Serves:** 4

455g ground chicken thigh meat
50g frozen spinach, thawed and drained
35g crumbled feta
¼ teaspoon onion powder
½ teaspoon garlic powder
230g pork rinds, finely ground

1 Mix all ingredients in a large bowl and roll the mixture into 2" balls. 2. Insert the crisper plate in the drawer in the lower position. Working in batches if needed, arrange the balls in a single layer in the drawer and insert the drawer into the unit. 3. Select AIR FRY, set the temperature to 175°C and set the time to 12 minutes. Select START/STOP to begin cooking. 4. When done, internal temperature will be 75°C. Serve immediately.

Chapter 4 Poultry

Garlic Chicken Wings with Green Beans and Rice

⏲ **Prep Time: 10 minutes** 🍲 **Cook: 40 minutes** 🍽 **Serves: 4**

185g long-grain white rice, rinsed and drained
110g cut frozen green beans (do not thaw)
1 tablespoon minced fresh ginger
3 cloves garlic, minced
1 tablespoon toasted sesame oil
1 teaspoon kosher salt
1 teaspoon black pepper
455g chicken wings, preferably drumettes

1. In a round heatproof pan, combine the rice, ginger, garlic, sesame oil, salt, green beans, and pepper. Stir to combine. Place the chicken wings on top of the rice mixture. 2. Cover the pan with foil and make a long slash in the foil to allow the pan to vent steam. 3. Insert the crisper plate in the drawer in the lower position, place the pan in the drawer, and insert the drawer into the unit. 4. Select AIR FRY, set the temperature to 190°C and set the time to 30 minutes. Select START/STOP to begin cooking. 5. Remove the foil and cook at 200°C for 10 minutes, or until the wings have browned and rendered fat into the rice and vegetables, turning the wings halfway through the cooking time. 6. When done, serve and enjoy.

Spicy Black Bean Turkey Burgers with Avocado Spread

⏲ **Prep Time: 10 minutes** 🍲 **Cook: 20 minutes** 🍽 **Serves: 2**

255g canned black beans, drained and rinsed
315g lean ground turkey
2 tablespoons minced red onion
1 jalapeño pepper, seeded and minced
2 tablespoons plain breadcrumbs
½ teaspoon chilli powder
¼ teaspoon cayenne pepper
Salt, to taste
Olive or vegetable oil
2 slices pepper jack cheese
Toasted burger rolls, sliced tomatoes, lettuce leaves

Cumin-Avocado Spread:

1 ripe avocado
Juice of 1 lime
1 teaspoon ground cumin
½ teaspoon salt
1 tablespoon chopped fresh cilantro
Freshly ground black pepper

1. Place the black beans in a large bowl and smash slightly with the back of a fork. Add the Jalapeño pepper, ground turkey, red onion, breadcrumbs, chilli powder, and cayenne pepper. Season with the salt. Mix all the ingredients with your hands and shape them into 2 patties. Brush both sides of the burger patties with a little olive or vegetable oil. 2. Insert the crisper plate in the drawer in the lower position, place the burgers in the drawer, and insert the drawer into the unit. 3. Select AIR FRY, set the temperature to 195°C and set the time to 20 minutes. Select START/STOP to begin cooking. Cook, flipping over halfway through the cooking process. During the last 2 minutes of the cooking process, top the burgers with pepper jack cheese (use toothpicks to secure the cheese slices to the burgers). 4. While the burgers are cooking, make the cumin avocado spread. Place the avocado, cumin, lime juice, and salt in food processor and process until smooth. (For a chunkier spread, you can mash this by hand in a bowl.) Stir in the cilantro and season with the freshly ground black pepper. Refrigerate the spread until you are ready to serve. 5. When the burgers have finished cooking, remove and let rest on a plate, covered gently with aluminium foil. 6. Brush the insides of the burger rolls with a little olive oil. Place the rolls, cut side up, into the drawer and air-fry at 200°C for 1 minute to toast and warm them. 7. Spread the cumin-avocado spread on the rolls and build your burgers with the lettuce, sliced tomatoes, and any other ingredient you like. Serve warm.

Classic Nashville Hot Chicken

⏱ **Prep Time: 7 minutes**   🍳 **Cook: 20 minutes**   🍽 **Serves: 4**

1 (115g) chicken, cut into 6 pieces (2 breasts, 2 thighs and 2 drumsticks)
2 eggs
240ml buttermilk
240g all-purpose flour
2 tablespoons paprika
1 teaspoon garlic powder
1 teaspoon onion powder
2 teaspoons salt
1 teaspoon freshly ground black pepper
Vegetable oil, in a spray bottle

Nashville Hot Sauce:
1 tablespoon cayenne pepper
1 teaspoon salt
60ml vegetable oil
4 slices white bread
Dill pickle slices

1. Cut the chicken breasts into 2 pieces so that there are 8 pieces of chicken in total. 2. Set up a two-stage dredging station. In a bowl, whisk together the eggs and buttermilk. In a zipper-sealable plastic bag, combine the flour, onion powder, salt, paprika, garlic powder, and black pepper. Dip the chicken pieces into the egg and buttermilk mixture, then toss in the seasoned flour, coating all sides of the pieces. Repeat this step (dipping in the egg mixture and then flour mixture) one more time. This can be a little messy, but make sure all sides of the chicken are completely covered. Spray the chicken with the vegetable oil and set aside. 3. Insert the crisper plate in the drawer in the lower position and spray or brush the crisper plate with a little vegetable oil. 4. Working in two batches, arrange the chicken in a single layer in the drawer and insert the drawer into the unit. 5. Select AIR FRY, set the temperature to 185°C and set the time to 20 minutes. Select START/STOP to begin cooking. Cook, flipping the chicken pieces over halfway through the cooking process. 6. Transfer the chicken to a plate, but do not cover. Repeat with the second batch of chicken. 7. Lower the temperature on the air fryer to 170°C. Turn the chicken over and place the first batch of chicken on top of the second batch already in the drawer. Air fry for another 7 minutes. 8. While the chicken is air frying, mix the cayenne pepper with salt in a bowl. Heat the vegetable oil in a small saucepan. When the oil is very hot, add to the spice mix and stir until smooth. It will sizzle briefly when you add the oil to the spices. 9. Place the fried chicken on top of the white bread slices and brush chicken with the hot sauce all. Top with the pickle slices and serve warm.

Maple Bacon Wrapped Chicken Breasts

⏱ **Prep Time: 10 minutes**   🍳 **Cook: 18 minutes**   🍽 **Serves: 2**

2 (170g) boneless, skinless chicken breasts
2 tablespoons maple syrup, divided
Freshly ground black pepper
6 slices thick-sliced bacon
Fresh celery or parsley leaves

Ranch Dressing:
55g mayonnaise
60ml buttermilk
80g Greek yoghurt
1 tablespoon chopped fresh chives
1 tablespoon chopped fresh parsley
1 tablespoon chopped fresh dill
1 tablespoon lemon juice
Salt and freshly ground black pepper

1. Brush the chicken breasts with half the maple syrup and season with the freshly ground black pepper. Wrap three slices of bacon around each chicken breast, securing the ends with toothpicks. 2. Insert the crisper plate in the drawer in the lower position, place the chicken in the drawer, and insert the drawer into the unit. 3. Select AIR FRY, set the temperature to 195°C and set the time to 6 minutes. Select START/STOP to begin cooking. 4. Then turn the chicken breasts over, pour more maple syrup on top, and air-fry for another 6 minutes. Turn the chicken breasts one more time, brush the remaining maple syrup all over and continue to air-fry for a final 6 minutes. 5. While the chicken is cooking, prepare the dressing by combining all the dressing ingredients together in a bowl. 6. When the chicken has finished cooking, remove the toothpicks and serve each breast with a little dressing drizzled over each one. Scatter lots of fresh celery or parsley leaves on top.

| Chapter 4 Poultry

Thai Courgette Turkey Meatballs

⏱ Prep Time: 10 minutes 🍳 Cook: 10-12 minutes 🍽 Serves: 4-6

180g grated courgette,
Squeezed dry in a clean kitchen towel (about 1 large courgette)
3 scallions, finely chopped
2 cloves garlic, minced
1 tablespoon grated fresh ginger
1 tablespoon finely chopped fresh cilantro
Zest of 1 lime
1 teaspoon salt
Freshly ground black pepper
680g ground turkey (a mix of light and dark meat)
2 eggs, lightly beaten
170g Thai sweet chilli sauce (spring roll sauce)
Lime wedges, for serving

1. Combine the courgette, scallions, cilantro, lime zest, salt, garlic, ginger, pepper, ground turkey and eggs in a bowl and mix the ingredients together. Gently shape the mixture into 24 balls, about the size of golf balls. 2. Insert the crisper plate in the drawer in the lower position. Working in batches, arrange the meatballs in a single layer in the drawer and insert the drawer into the unit. 3. Select AIR FRY, set the temperature to 195°C and set the time to 10 minutes. Select START/STOP to begin cooking. Cook the meatballs for 10 to 12 minutes, turning over halfway through the cooking time. 4. As soon as the meatballs have finished cooking, toss them in a bowl with the Thai sweet chilli sauce to coat. 5. Serve the meatballs over rice noodles or white rice with the remaining Thai sweet chilli sauce and lime wedges to squeeze over the top.

Teriyaki Chicken Drumsticks

⏱ Prep Time: 10 minutes 🍳 Cook: 17 minutes 🍽 Serves: 2

2 tablespoons soy sauce
60ml dry sherry
1 tablespoon brown sugar
2 tablespoons water
1 tablespoon rice wine vinegar
1 clove garlic, crushed
1-inch fresh ginger, peeled and sliced
Pinch crushed red pepper flakes
4 to 6 bone-in, skin-on chicken drumsticks
1 tablespoon cornstarch
Fresh cilantro leaves

1. Make the marinade by combining the soy sauce, water, brown sugar, dry sherry, rice vinegar, garlic, ginger, and crushed red pepper flakes. Pour the marinade over the chicken legs, cover, and let the chicken marinate for 1 to 4 hours in the refrigerator. 2. Insert the crisper plate in the drawer in the lower position and transfer the chicken from the marinade to the drawer transferring any extra marinade to a small saucepan. Insert the drawer into the unit. 3. Select AIR FRY, set the temperature to 195°C and set the time to 8 minutes. Select START/STOP to begin cooking. 4. Flip the chicken over and continue to air-fry for another 6 minutes, watching to make sure it doesn't brown too much. 5. While the chicken is cooking, bring the reserved marinade to a simmer on the stovetop. Dissolve the cornstarch in 2 tablespoons of water and stir this into the saucepan. Bring to a boil to thicken the sauce. Remove the garlic clove and slices of ginger from the sauce and set aside. 6. When the time is up on the air fryer, brush the thickened sauce on the chicken and air-fry for 3 more minutes. Remove the chicken from the air fryer and brush with the remaining sauce. 7. Serve over rice and sprinkle the cilantro leaves on top.

Garlic Butter Chicken

⏱ **Prep Time: 10 minutes** 🍱 **Cook: 27 minutes** ❖ **Serves: 4**

2 tablespoon extra-virgin olive oil
1 tablespoon Dijon mustard
1 tablespoon apple cider vinegar
3 cloves garlic, minced
2 teaspoons herbes de Provence
½ teaspoon kosher salt
1 teaspoon black pepper
455g boneless, skinless chicken thighs, halved crosswise
2 tablespoons butter
8 cloves garlic, chopped
60g heavy whipping cream

1. In a small bowl, combine the olive oil, mustard, vinegar, herbes de Provence, salt, minced garlic, and pepper. Use a wire whisk to emulsify the mixture. 2. Pierce the chicken all over with a fork to allow the marinade to penetrate better. Place the chicken in a resealable plastic bag, pour the marinade over, and seal. Massage until the chicken is well coated. Marinate at room temperature for 30 minutes or in the refrigerator for up to 24 hours. 3. Insert the crisper plate in the drawer in the lower position. When you are ready to cook, place the butter and chopped garlic in a 7 × 3-inch round heatproof pan and place it in the drawer. Insert the drawer into the unit. Select ROAST, set the temperature to 200°C and set the time for 5 minutes. Select START/STOP to begin cooking. Cook until the butter has melted and the garlic is sizzling. 4. Add the chicken and the marinade to the seasoned butter. Set the air fryer to 175°C for 15 minutes. Use a meat thermometer to ensure the chicken has reached an internal temperature of 75°C. Transfer the chicken to a plate and cover lightly with foil to keep warm. 5. Add the cream to the pan, stirring to combine with the garlic, butter, and cooking juices. Place the pan in the drawer. Set the air fryer to 175°C for 7 minutes. 6. Pour the thickened sauce over the chicken and serve.

Marinated Ginger Chicken

⏱ **Prep Time: 10 minutes** 🍱 **Cook: 10 minutes** ❖ **Serves: 4**

25g julienned peeled fresh ginger
2 tablespoons vegetable oil
1 tablespoon honey
1 tablespoon soy sauce
1 tablespoon ketchup
1 teaspoon Garam Masala
1 teaspoon ground turmeric
¼ teaspoon kosher salt
½ teaspoon cayenne pepper
Vegetable oil spray
455g boneless, skinless chicken thighs, cut crosswise into thirds
5g chopped fresh coriander, for garnish

1. In a small bowl, combine the ginger, oil, honey, garam masala, turmeric, salt, soy sauce, ketchup, and cayenne. Whisk until well combined. Place the chicken in a resealable plastic bag and pour the marinade over. Seal the bag and massage to cover all of the chicken with the marinade. Marinate at room temperature for 30 minutes or in the refrigerator for up to 24 hours. 2. Insert the crisper plate in the drawer in the lower position and spray the crisper plate with the vegetable oil spray and add the chicken and as much of the marinade and julienned ginger as possible in the drawer. Insert the drawer into the unit. Select ROAST, set the temperature to 175°C and set the time for 10 minutes. Select START/STOP to begin cooking. Use a meat thermometer to ensure the chicken has reached an internal temperature of 75°C. 3. To serve, garnish the chicken with the coriander.

Chapter 5 Fish and Seafood

44 Nutritious Cucumber and Salmon Salad
44 Crispy Coconut Shrimp
45 Low-Carb Tuna Patties with Spicy Sriracha Sauce
45 Sesame-Crusted Salmon
46 Crispy Fish Sticks with Tartar Sauce
46 Chinese Ginger-Scallion Fish
47 Delicious Bang Bang Shrimp
47 Lime Shrimp with Garlic Peanuts
48 Homemade Crispy Fish and Chips
48 Crispy Buttermilk Catfish Strips
49 Homestyle Fish Sticks
49 Easy Tuna Patty Sliders
50 Blackened Shrimp Tacos with Coleslaw
50 Hearty Crab Stuffed Salmon Roast
51 Roasted Chilean Sea Bass with Olive Relish
51 Spicy Orange Shrimp

Nutritious Cucumber and Salmon Salad

⏰ **Prep Time: 10 minutes**   🍲 **Cook: 8-10 minutes**   ◈ **Serves: 2**

455g salmon fillet
1½ tablespoons olive oil, divided
1 tablespoon sherry vinegar
1 tablespoon capers, rinsed and drained
1 seedless cucumber, thinly sliced
¼ Vidalia onion, thinly sliced
2 tablespoons chopped fresh parsley
Salt and freshly ground black pepper

1. Lightly coat the salmon with ½ tablespoon of the olive oil. 2. Insert the crisper plate in the drawer in the lower position, place the salmon skin-side down in the drawer, and insert the drawer into the unit. 3. Select AIR FRY, set the temperature to 200°C and set the time to 8 minutes. Select START/STOP to begin cooking. Air fry for 8 to 10 minutes until the fish is opaque and flakes easily with a fork. 4. Transfer the salmon to a plate and let cool to room temperature. Remove the skin and carefully flake the fish into bite-size chunks. 5. In a small bowl, whisk the remaining 1 tablespoon olive oil and the vinegar until thoroughly combined. Add the flaked fish, cucumber, capers, onion, and parsley. Season to taste with the salt and freshly ground black pepper. Toss gently to coat. Serve immediately, or cover and refrigerate for up to 4 hours.

Crispy Coconut Shrimp

⏰ **Prep Time: 5 minutes**   🍲 **Cook: 6 minutes**   ◈ **Serves: 2**

230g medium shelled and deveined shrimp
2 tablespoons salted butter, melted
½ teaspoon Old Bay seasoning
20g unsweetened shredded coconut

1. In a large bowl, toss the shrimp in butter and Old Bay seasoning. 2. Place shredded coconut in the bowl and coat each piece of shrimp in the coconut. 3. Insert the crisper plate in the drawer in the lower position, place the shrimp in the drawer, and insert the drawer into the unit. 4. Select AIR FRY, set the temperature to 200°C and set the time to 6 minutes. Select START/STOP to begin cooking. Gently turn the shrimp halfway through the cooking time. 5. Serve immediately.

Low-Carb Tuna Patties with Spicy Sriracha Sauce

⏲ **Prep Time: 10 minutes** 🍴 **Cook: 10 minutes** ❖ **Serves: 4**

2 (170g) cans tuna packed in oil, drained
3 tablespoons almond flour
2 tablespoons mayonnaise
1 teaspoon dried dill
½ teaspoon onion powder
Pinch of salt and pepper

Spicy Sriracha Sauce:
55g mayonnaise
1 tablespoon sriracha sauce
1 teaspoon garlic powder

1. Insert the crisper plate in the drawer in the lower position and line the crisper plate with parchment paper. 2. In a large bowl, combine the tuna, dill, mayonnaise, almond flour, and onion powder. Season to taste with the salt and freshly ground black pepper. Use a fork to stir, mashing with the back of the fork as necessary, until thoroughly combined. 3. Form the tuna mixture patties with an ice cream scoop. Place the patties in a single layer on the parchment paper in the drawer. Press lightly with the bottom of the scoop to flatten into a circle about ½ inch thick. Insert the drawer into the unit. 4. Select AIR FRY, set the temperature to 195°C and set the time to 10 minutes. Select START/STOP to begin cooking. Cook until lightly browned, pausing halfway through the cooking time to turn the patties. 5. Make the sriracha sauce by combining the sriracha, mayonnaise, and garlic powder in a small bowl. Serve the tuna patties topped with the sriracha sauce.

Sesame-Crusted Salmon

⏲ **Prep Time: 10 minutes** 🍴 **Cook: 10 minutes** ❖ **Serves: 4**

80g mixed black and brown sesame seeds
1 tablespoon reduced-sodium soy sauce
1 teaspoon sesame oil
1 teaspoon honey
4 (170g) salmon fillets, skin removed
2 tablespoons chopped fresh marjoram, for garnish (optional)

1. Place the sesame seeds on a plate or in a small shallow bowl. In a separate small bowl, combine the soy sauce, sesame oil, and honey. 2. Brush all sides of the salmon with the soy sauce mixture until thoroughly coated. Press the top of each fillet into the sesame seeds to create a coating. 3. Insert the crisper plate in the drawer in the lower position, place the fish seed-side up in a single layer in the drawer, and insert the drawer into the unit. 4. Select AIR FRY, set the temperature to 180°C and set the time to 10 minutes. Select START/STOP to begin cooking. Cook until the fish is firm and flakes easily with a fork. 5. Top with the marjoram, if desired, serve and enjoy.

Crispy Fish Sticks with Tartar Sauce

⏱ **Prep Time: 10 minutes** 🍳 **Cook: 6 minutes** ≋ **Serves: 2-3**

340g cod or flounder
60g flour
½ teaspoon paprika
1 teaspoon salt
Lots of freshly ground black pepper
2 eggs, lightly beaten
165g panko breadcrumbs
1 teaspoon salt
Vegetable oil

Tartar Sauce:

55g mayonnaise
2 teaspoons lemon juice
2 tablespoons finely chopped sweet pickles
Salt and freshly ground black pepper

1. Cut the fish into ¾-inch wide strips or sticks. Set up a dredging station. Combine the flour, salt, paprika, and pepper in a shallow dish. Lightly beat the eggs in a second shallow dish. Mix the breadcrumbs and salt in a third shallow dish. 2. Dip the fish into the flour, then into the egg, and finally into the breadcrumbs, coating on all sides in each step and pressing the crumbs firmly onto the fish. Place the finished sticks on a baking sheet or plate while you finish all the sticks and spray the fish sticks with the oil. 3. Insert the crisper plate in the drawer in the lower position and spray or brush the crisper plate with the oil. Place the fish into the drawer and insert the drawer into the unit. 4. Select AIR FRY, set the temperature to 200°C and set the time to 4 minutes. Select START/STOP to begin cooking. 5. Turn the fish sticks over and air-fry for another 2 minutes. 6. While the fish is cooking, mix the tartar sauce ingredients together. 7. Serve the fish sticks warm with the tartar sauce and some French fries on the side.

Chinese Ginger-Scallion Fish

⏱ **Prep Time: 15 minutes** 🍳 **Cook: 15 minutes** ≋ **Serves: 2**

For the Bean Sauce:

2 tablespoons soy sauce
1 tablespoon rice wine
1 tablespoon doubanjiang (Chinese black bean paste)
1 teaspoon minced fresh ginger
1 clove garlic, minced

For the Vegetables and Fish:

1 tablespoon peanut oil
25g julienned green onions (white and green parts)
5g chopped fresh cilantro
2 tablespoons julienned fresh ginger
2 (170g) white fish fillets, such as tilapia

For the sauce: 1. In a small bowl, combine all the ingredients and stir until well combined; set aside.
For the vegetables and fish: 1. In a medium bowl, combine the peanut oil, green onions, cilantro, and ginger. Toss to combine. 2. Cut two squares of parchment large enough to hold one fillet and half of the vegetables. Place one fillet on each parchment square, top with the vegetables, and pour over the sauce. Fold over the parchment paper and crimp the sides in small, tight folds to hold the fish, vegetables, and sauce securely inside the packet. 3. Insert the crisper plate in the drawer in the lower position, place the packets in a single layer in the drawer, and insert the drawer into the unit. 4. Select AIR FRY, set the temperature to 175°C and set the time to 15 minutes. Select START/STOP to begin cooking. 5. Transfer each packet to a dinner plate. Cut open with scissors just before serving.

Chapter 5 Fish and Seafood

Delicious Bang Bang Shrimp

⏱ Prep Time: 15 minutes 🍲 Cook: 14 minutes 🍽 Serves: 4

For the Sauce:
110g mayonnaise
40g sweet chilli sauce
2 to 4 tablespoons sriracha
1 teaspoon minced fresh ginger

For the Shrimp:
455g jumbo raw shrimp (21 to 25 count), peeled and deveined
2 tablespoons cornstarch or rice flour
½ teaspoon kosher salt
Vegetable oil spray

For the sauce: 1. In a large bowl, combine the mayonnaise, chilli sauce, sriracha, and ginger. Stir until well combined. Remove half of the sauce to serve as a dipping sauce.
For the shrimp: 1. Place the shrimp in a medium bowl. Sprinkle the cornstarch and salt over the shrimp and toss until well coated. 2. Insert the crisper plate in the drawer in the lower position, place the shrimp in a single layer in the drawer. (If they won't fit in a single layer, set a rack or trivet on top of the bottom layer of shrimp and place the rest of the shrimp on the rack.) Spray generously with vegetable oil spray and insert the drawer into the unit. 3. Select AIR FRY, set the temperature to 175°C and set the time to 10 minutes. Select START/STOP to begin cooking. 4. Turn and spray with additional oil spray halfway through the cooking time. 5. Remove the shrimp and toss in the bowl with half of the sauce. Place the shrimp back in the drawer and cook at 175°C for an additional 4 to 5 minutes, or until the sauce has formed a glaze. 6. Serve the hot shrimp with the reserved sauce for dipping.

Lime Shrimp with Garlic Peanuts

⏱ Prep Time: 15 minutes 🍲 Cook: 10 minutes 🍽 Serves: 4

For the Peanut Mix:
60g roasted and salted red-skinned Spanish peanuts
8 cloves garlic, smashed and peeled
3 dried red arbol chillis, broken into pieces
1 tablespoon cumin seeds
2 teaspoons vegetable oil

For the Shrimp:
455g jumbo raw shrimp (21 to 25 count), peeled and deveined
2 tablespoons vegetable oil
Lime wedges, for serving

For the peanut mix: 1. In a round heatproof pan, combine all the ingredients and toss. 2. Place the pan in the drawer and insert the drawer into the unit. 3. Select BAKE, set the temperature to 200°C and set the time for 5 minutes. Select START/STOP to begin cooking. Cook until all the spices are toasted. Remove the pan from the drawer and let the mixture cool. 4. When completely cool, transfer the mixture to a mortar and pestle or clean coffee or spice grinder and crush or pulse to a very coarse texture.
For the shrimp: 1. In a large bowl, combine the shrimp and oil. Toss until well combined. Add the peanut mix and toss again. Place the shrimp and peanut mix in the drawer and cook at 175°C for 5 minutes. 2. Transfer to a serving dish. Cover and allow the shrimp to finish cooking in the residual heat, about 5 minutes. Serve with the lime wedges.

| Chapter 5 Fish and Seafood

Homemade Crispy Fish and Chips

Prep Time: 25 minutes   Cook: 35 minutes   Serves: 4

For the Chips:
1 tablespoon olive oil, plus more for spraying
2 large russet potatoes, scrubbed
1 teaspoon salt
½ teaspoon freshly ground black pepper

For the Fish:
Olive oil
4 (115g) cod fillets
1½ teaspoons salt, divided plus more as needed
1½ teaspoons black pepper, divided, plus more as needed
60g whole-wheat flour
2 eggs
165g whole-wheat panko bread crumbs
¼ teaspoon cayenne pepper

To make the chips: 1. Insert the crisper plate in the drawer in the lower position and spray the crisper plate with the olive oil. 2. Cut the potatoes lengthwise into ½-inch-thick slices and then into ½-inch-thick fries. 3. In a large bowl, mix together the oil, salt, and pepper and toss with the potatoes to coat. 4. Place the potatoes in a single layer in the drawer. You may need to cook them in batches. Insert the drawer into the unit. 5. Select AIR FRY, set the temperature to 200°C and set the time to 5 minutes. Select START/STOP to begin cooking. 6. Remove the drawer, shake, and cook until the potatoes are lightly browned and crisp, 5 to 10 more minutes. 7. Set aside and keep warm.

To make the fish: 1. Insert the crisper plate in the drawer in the lower position and spray the crisper plate with the olive oil. 2. Season the fillets with the salt and black pepper. 3. In a shallow bowl, mix together the whole-wheat flour, ½ teaspoon of salt, and ½ teaspoon of black pepper. 4. In a second bowl, whisk together the eggs, 1 teaspoon of water, and a pinch of salt and pepper. 5. In another shallow bowl, combine the cayenne pepper, panko bread crumbs, and remaining 1 teaspoon of salt and 1 teaspoon of black pepper. 6. Coat each fillet in the seasoned flour, then coat with the egg, and dredge in the panko bread crumb mixture. 7. Place the fillets in the drawer in a single layer and lightly spray the fish with olive oil. You may need to cook them in batches. Insert the drawer into the unit. 8. Air fry at 200°C for 8 to 10 minutes. 9. Turn the fillets over and lightly spray with the olive oil. Cook until golden brown and crispy, 5 to 10 more minutes. 10. When done, serve the fish with chips.

Crispy Buttermilk Catfish Strips

Prep Time: 15 minutes   Cook: 20 minutes   Serves: 4

240ml buttermilk
5 catfish fillets, cut into 1½-inch strips
Olive oil
130g cornmeal
1 tablespoon Creole, Cajun, or Old Bay seasoning

1. Pour the buttermilk into a shallow baking dish. Place the catfish in the dish and refrigerate for at least 1 hour to help remove any fishy taste. 2. Insert the crisper plate in the drawer in the lower position and lightly spray the crisper plate with the olive oil. 3. In a shallow bowl, combine cornmeal and Creole seasoning. 4. Shake any excess buttermilk off the catfish. Place each strip in the cornmeal mixture and coat completely. Press the cornmeal into the catfish gently to help it stick. 5. Place the strips in the drawer in a single layer and lightly spray the catfish with the olive oil. You may need to cook the catfish in more than one batch. Insert the drawer into the unit. 6. Select AIR FRY, set the temperature to 200°C and set the time to 8 minutes. Select START/STOP to begin cooking. 7. Turn the catfish strips over and lightly spray with the olive oil. Cook until golden brown and crispy, 8 to 10 more minutes. 8. When done, serve and enjoy.

Chapter 5 Fish and Seafood | 48

Homestyle Fish Sticks

⏰ **Prep Time:** 15 minutes 🍲 **Cook:** 15 minutes ≋ **Serves:** 4

Olive oil
4 fish fillets (cod, tilapia or pollock)
60g whole-wheat flour
1 teaspoon seasoned salt
2 eggs
165g whole-wheat panko bread crumbs
½ tablespoon dried parsley flakes

1. Insert the crisper plate in the drawer in the lower position and lightly spray the crisper plate with the olive oil. 2. Cut the fish fillets lengthwise into "sticks." 3. In a shallow bowl, mix together the whole-wheat flour and seasoned salt. 4. In a small bowl whisk the eggs with 1 teaspoon of water. 5. In another shallow bowl, mix together the panko bread crumbs and parsley flakes. 6. Coat each fish stick in the seasoned flour, then in the egg mixture, and dredge them in the panko bread crumbs. 7. Place the fish sticks in the drawer in a single layer and lightly spray the fish sticks with the olive oil. You may need to cook them in batches. Insert the drawer into the unit. 8. Select AIR FRY, set the temperature to 200°C and set the time to 5 minutes. Select START/STOP to begin cooking. Air fry for 5 to 8 minutes. 9. Flip the fish sticks over and lightly spray with the olive oil. Cook until golden brown and crispy, 5 to 7 more minutes. 10. When done, serve and enjoy.

Easy Tuna Patty Sliders

⏰ **Prep Time:** 15 minutes 🍲 **Cook:** 15 minutes ≋ **Serves:** 4

Olive oil
3 (140g) cans tuna, packed in water
75g whole-wheat panko bread crumbs
35g shredded Parmesan cheese
1 tablespoon sriracha
¾ teaspoon black pepper
10 whole-wheat slider buns

1. Insert the crisper plate in the drawer in the lower position and lightly spray the crisper plate with the olive oil. 2. In a medium bowl combine the tuna, bread crumbs, sriracha, Parmesan cheese, and black pepper and stir to combine. 3. Form the mixture into 10 patties. 4. Place the patties in the drawer in a single layer and spray the patties lightly with the olive oil. You may need to cook them in batches. Insert the drawer into the unit. 5. Select AIR FRY, set the temperature to 175°C and set the time to 6 minutes. Select START/STOP to begin cooking. Air fry for 6 to 8 minutes. 6. Turn the patties over and lightly spray with the olive oil. Cook until golden brown and crisp, another 4 to 7 more minutes. 7. Serve on whole-wheat buns.

Chapter 5 Fish and Seafood

Blackened Shrimp Tacos with Coleslaw

Prep Time: 10 minutes   Cook: 10-15 minutes   Serves: 4

1 teaspoon olive oil, plus more for spraying
340g medium shrimp, deveined, tails off
1 to 2 teaspoons blackened seasoning
8 corn tortillas, warmed
1 (400g) bag coleslaw mix
2 limes, cut in half

1. Insert the crisper plate in the drawer in the lower position and lightly spray the crisper plate with the olive oil. 2. Dry the shrimp with a paper towel to remove excess water. 3. In a medium bowl, toss the shrimp with 1 teaspoon of olive oil and blackened seasoning. 4. Place the shrimp in the drawer and cook for 5 minutes. 5. Select AIR FRY, set the temperature to 200°C and set the time to 5 minutes. Select START/STOP to begin cooking. 6. Remove the drawer to shake, lightly spray with the olive oil, and cook until the shrimp are cooked through and starting to brown, 5 to 10 more minutes. 7. Fill each tortilla with the coleslaw mix and top with the blackened shrimp. Squeeze fresh lime juice over top. Serve and enjoy.

Hearty Crab Stuffed Salmon Roast

Prep Time: 10 minutes   Cook: 20 minutes   Serves: 4-6

1 (680g) salmon fillet
Salt and freshly ground black pepper
170g crabmeat
1 teaspoon finely chopped lemon zest
1 teaspoon Dijon mustard
1 tablespoon chopped fresh parsley, plus more for garnish
1 scallion, chopped
¼ teaspoon salt
Olive oil

1. Prepare the salmon fillet by butterflying it. Slice into the thickest side of the salmon, parallel to the countertop and along the length of the fillet. Don't slice all the way through to the other side – stop about an inch from the edge. Open the salmon up like a book. Season the salmon with the salt and freshly ground black pepper. 2. Make the crab filling by combining the crabmeat, mustard, parsley, scallion, salt, lemon zest, and freshly ground black pepper in a bowl. Spread this filling in the centre of the salmon. Fold one side of the salmon over the filling. Then fold the other side over on top. 3. Transfer the rolled salmon to the centre of a piece of parchment paper that is roughly 6- to 7-inches wide and about 12-inches long. The parchment paper will act as a sling, making it easier to put the salmon into the drawer. 4. Insert the crisper plate in the drawer in the lower position. Use the parchment paper to transfer the salmon roast to the drawer and tuck the ends of the paper down beside the salmon. Drizzle a little olive oil on top and season with the salt and pepper. Insert the drawer into the unit. 5. Select AIR FRY, set the temperature to 185°C and set the time to 20 minutes. Select START/STOP to begin cooking. 6. Remove the roast from the air fryer and let it rest for a few minutes. Then, slice it, sprinkle some more lemon zest and parsley (or fresh chives) on top and serve.

Roasted Chilean Sea Bass with Olive Relish

⏰ **Prep Time: 10 minutes** 🍲 **Cook: 10 minutes** 🍽 **Serves: 2**

Olive oil spray
2 (170g) Chilean sea bass fillets or other firm-fleshed white fish
3 tablespoons extra-virgin olive oil
½ teaspoon ground cumin
½ teaspoon kosher salt
½ teaspoon black pepper
45g pitted green olives, diced
30g finely diced onion
1 teaspoon chopped capers

1. Insert the crisper plate in the drawer in the lower position and spray the crisper plate with the olive oil spray. 2. Drizzle the fillets with the olive oil and sprinkle with the cumin, salt, and pepper. 3. Place the fish in the drawer and insert the drawer into the unit. 4. Select ROAST, set the temperature to 160°C and set the time to 10 minutes. Select START/STOP to begin cooking. Cook or until the fish flakes easily with a fork. 5. Meanwhile, in a small bowl, stir together the olives, onion, and capers. 6. Serve the fish topped with the relish.

Spicy Orange Shrimp

⏰ **Prep Time: 40 minutes** 🍲 **Cook: 15 minutes** 🍽 **Serves: 4**

Olive oil
80ml orange juice
3 teaspoons minced garlic
1 teaspoon Old Bay seasoning
¼ to ½ teaspoon cayenne pepper
455g medium shrimp, thawed, deveined, peeled, with tails off

1. In a medium bowl, combine the orange juice, garlic, Old Bay seasoning, and cayenne pepper. 2. Dry the shrimp with paper towels to remove excess water. 3. Add the shrimp to the marinade and stir to evenly coat. Cover with plastic wrap and place in the refrigerator for 30 minutes so the shrimp can soak up the marinade. 4. Insert the crisper plate in the drawer in the lower position and spray the crisper plate lightly with the olive oil. Place the shrimp into the drawer and insert the drawer into the unit. 5. Select AIR FRY, set the temperature to 200°C and set the time to 5 minutes. Select START/STOP to begin cooking. 6. Shake the drawer and lightly spray with olive oil. Cook until the shrimp are opaque and crisp, 5 to 10 more minutes. 7. When done, serve and enjoy.

Chapter 5 Fish and Seafood | 51

Chapter 6 Beef and Pork

53 Honey Lemon Roasted Pork Loin
53 Country-Style Barbecue Ribs
54 Crispy Chinese Five-Spice Pork Belly
54 Spicy Pork Tenderloin with Avocado Lime Sauce
55 Air Fried Barbecued Riblets
55 Peppercorn-Crusted Beef Tenderloin
56 Crispy Breaded Pork Chops
56 Beef Lasagna Casserole
57 Marinated Steak Tips with Mushrooms
57 Beef Meatballs and Spaghetti Zoodles
58 Air-Fried Rib Eye Steaks with Horseradish Cream
58 Guacamole Bacon Burgers
59 Chinese-Style Spareribs
59 Blue Cheese and Steak Salad with Balsamic Vinaigrette
60 Glazed Ham Steaks with Sweet Potatoes
60 Spicy Baby Back Ribs

Honey Lemon Roasted Pork Loin

⏲ Prep Time: 10 minutes   🍲 Cook: 22-25 minutes   ◈ Serves: 6

85g honey
60ml freshly squeezed lemon juice
2 tablespoons soy sauce
1 teaspoon garlic powder
1 (910g) pork loin
2 tablespoons vegetable oil

1. In a medium bowl, whisk together the honey, soy sauce, lemon juice, and garlic powder. Reserve half of the mixture for basting during cooking. 2. Cut 5 slits in the pork loin and transfer it to a resealable bag. Add the remaining honey mixture. Seal the bag and refrigerate to marinate for at least 2 hours. 3. Insert the crisper plate in the drawer in the lower position and line the crisper plate with parchment paper. 4. Remove the pork from the marinade and place it on the parchment. Spritz with oil and baste with the reserved marinade. Insert the drawer into the unit. 5. Select ROAST, set the temperature to 200°C and set the time for 15 minutes. Select START/STOP to begin cooking. 6. Flip the pork, baste with more marinade, and spritz with oil again. Cook for 7 to 10 minutes more until the internal temperature reaches 60°C. 7. Let rest for 5 minutes before serving. You can drizzle with more marinade if desired.

Country-Style Barbecue Ribs

⏲ Prep Time: 10 minutes   🍲 Cook: 15 minutes   ◈ Serves: 4

480ml cola
3 tablespoons light brown sugar
2 teaspoons garlic powder
2 teaspoons paprika
2 teaspoons Italian-Style Seasoning
1 teaspoon salt
½ teaspoon freshly ground black pepper
910g boneless pork ribs
500g Peachy Barbecue Sauce

1. In a medium bowl, stir together the cola, garlic powder, brown sugar, paprika, Italian-Style Seasoning, salt, and pepper. Reserve 120ml of the cola mixture for basting during cooking. 2. In a large resealable plastic bag, combine the remaining cola mixture and the ribs. Seal the bag and refrigerate to marinate for 8 hours. Remove the ribs from the cola mixture. 3. Insert the crisper plate in the drawer in the lower position and line the crisper plate with parchment paper. 4. Place the ribs on the parchment and brush with the reserved cola mixture. 5. Select AIR FRY, set the temperature to 175°C and set the time to 6 minutes. Select START/STOP to begin cooking. 6. Flip the ribs and baste with the cola mixture. Cook for 7 to 9 minutes more until the internal temperature reaches 60°C. 7. Let sit for 2 to 3 minutes before serving with the peachy barbecue sauce.

Crispy Chinese Five-Spice Pork Belly

Prep Time: 10 minutes   Cook: 17 minutes   Serves: 4

455g unsalted pork belly
2 teaspoons Chinese five-spice powder

Sauce:
1 tablespoon coconut oil
1 (1-inch) piece fresh ginger, peeled and grated
2 cloves garlic, minced
120ml beef or chicken broth
15g to 30g Swerve confectioners'-style sweetener or equivalent amount of liquid or powdered sweetener
3 tablespoons wheat-free tamari, or 120g coconut aminos
1 green onion, sliced, plus more for garnish
1 drop orange oil, or ½ teaspoon orange extract (optional)

1. Insert the crisper plate in the drawer in the lower position and spray the crisper plate with the avocado oil. 2. Cut the pork belly into ½-inch-thick slices and season well on all sides with the five-spice powder. 3. Place the slices in a single layer in the drawer and insert the drawer into the unit. 4. Select AIR FRY, set the temperature to 200°C and set the time to 8 minutes. Select START/STOP to begin cooking. Cook until cooked to your liking, flipping halfway through. 5. While the pork belly cooks, make the sauce. Heat the coconut oil in a small saucepan over medium heat. Add the garlic and ginger and sauté for 1 minute, or until fragrant. Add the broth, sweetener, and tamari and simmer for 10 to 15 minutes, until thickened. Add the green onion and cook for another minute, until the green onion is softened. Add the orange oil (if using). Taste and adjust the seasoning to your liking. 6. Transfer the pork belly to a large bowl. Pour the sauce over the pork belly and coat well. Place the pork belly slices on a serving platter and garnish with the sliced green onions. 7. Best served fresh. Store leftovers in an airtight container in the fridge for up to 4 days. Reheat in a 200°C air fryer for 3 minutes, or until heated through.

Spicy Pork Tenderloin with Avocado Lime Sauce

Prep Time: 10 minutes   Cook: 15 minutes   Serves: 4

Marinade:
120ml lime juice
Grated zest of 1 lime
2 teaspoons stevia glycerite, or ¼ teaspoon liquid stevia
3 cloves garlic, minced
1½ teaspoons fine sea salt
1 teaspoon chilli powder, or more for more heat
1 teaspoon smoked paprika
455g pork tenderloin

Avocado Lime Sauce:
1 medium-sized ripe avocado, roughly chopped
115g full-fat sour cream (or coconut cream for dairy-free)
Grated zest of 1 lime
Juice of 1 lime
2 cloves garlic, roughly chopped
½ teaspoon fine sea salt
¼ teaspoon ground black pepper
Chopped fresh cilantro leaves, for garnish
Lime slices, for serving
Pico de gallo, for serving

1. In a medium-sized casserole dish, stir together all the marinade ingredients until well combined. Add the tenderloin and coat it well in the marinade. Cover and place in the fridge to marinate for 2 hours or overnight. 2. Insert the crisper plate in the drawer in the lower position and spray the crisper plate with the avocado oil. 3. Remove the pork from the marinade and place it in the drawer. Select AIR FRY, set the temperature to 200°C and set the time to 13 minutes. Select START/STOP to begin cooking. Cook for 13 to 15 minutes, until the internal temperature of the pork is 60°C, flipping after 7 minutes. 4. Remove the pork from the air fryer and place on a cutting board. Let rest for 8 to 10 minutes, then cut it into ½-inch-thick slices. 5. While the pork cooks, make the avocado lime sauce by placing all the sauce ingredients in a food processor and puree until smooth. Taste and adjust the seasoning to your liking. 6. Arrange the pork slices on a serving platter and spoon the avocado lime sauce on top. Garnish with the cilantro leaves and serve with the lime slices and pico de gallo. 7. Store leftovers in an airtight container in the fridge for up to 4 days. Reheat in a 200°C air fryer for 5 minutes, or until heated through.

Air Fried Barbecued Riblets

🕐 **Prep Time: 10 minutes** 🍳 **Cook: 25 minutes** ❖ **Serves: 4**

1 rack pork riblets, cut into individual riblets
1 teaspoon fine sea salt
1 teaspoon ground black pepper

Sauce:
60ml apple cider vinegar
60ml beef broth
15g Swerve confectioners'-style sweetener or equivalent amount of liquid or powdered sweetener
60g tomato sauce
1 teaspoon liquid smoke
1 teaspoon onion powder
2 cloves garlic, minced

1. Insert the crisper plate in the drawer in the lower position and spray the crisper plate with the avocado oil. 2. Season the riblets well on all sides with the salt and pepper. Place the riblets in the drawer and insert the drawer into the unit. 3. Select AIR FRY, set the temperature to 175°C and set the time to 10 minutes. Select START/STOP to begin cooking. Cook, flipping halfway through. 4. While the riblets cook, mix all the sauce ingredients together in a pie pan. 5. Remove the riblets from the air fryer and place them in the pie pan with the sauce. Stir to coat the riblets in the sauce. Transfer the pan to the drawer and cook at 175°C for 10 to 15 minutes, until the pork is cooked through and the internal temperature reaches 60°C. 6. Store leftovers in an airtight container in the refrigerator for up to 4 days. Reheat in a 175°C air fryer for 5 minutes, or until heated through.

Peppercorn-Crusted Beef Tenderloin

🕐 **Prep Time: 10 minutes** 🍳 **Cook: 25 minutes** ❖ **Serves: 6**

2 tablespoons salted butter, melted
2 teaspoons minced roasted garlic
3 tablespoons ground 4-peppercorn blend
1 (910g) beef tenderloin, trimmed of visible fat

1 In a small bowl, mix the butter and roasted garlic. Brush it over the beef tenderloin. 2 Place the ground peppercorns onto a plate and roll the tenderloin through them, creating a crust. 3. Insert the crisper plate in the drawer in the lower position, place the tenderloin in the drawer, and insert the drawer into the unit. 4. Select AIR FRY, set the temperature to 200°C and set the time to 25 minutes. Select START/STOP to begin cooking. 5. Turn the tenderloin halfway through the cooking time. 6. Allow the meat to rest for 10 minutes before slicing.

Chapter 6 Beef and Pork | 55

Crispy Breaded Pork Chops

⏰ **Prep Time: 10 minutes** 🍱 **Cook: 15 minutes** ◈ **Serves: 4**

45g pork rinds, finely ground
1 teaspoon chilli powder
½ teaspoon garlic powder
1 tablespoon coconut oil, melted
4 (115g) pork chops

1 In a large bowl, mix the ground pork rinds, chilli powder, and garlic powder. 2 Brush each pork chop with the coconut oil and then press into the pork rind mixture, coating both sides. 3. Insert the crisper plate in the drawer in the lower position, place the each coated pork chop in the drawer, and insert the drawer into the unit. 4. Select AIR FRY, set the temperature to 200°C and set the time to 15 minutes. Select START/STOP to begin cooking. 5. Flip each pork chop halfway through the cooking time. 6. When fully cooked, the pork chops will be golden on the outside and have an internal temperature of at least 60°C. serve and enjoy.

Beef Lasagna Casserole

⏰ **Prep Time: 15 minutes** 🍱 **Cook: 15 minutes** ◈ **Serves: 4**

160g low-carb no-sugar-added pasta sauce
455g 80/20 ground beef, cooked and drained
125g full-fat ricotta cheese
25g grated Parmesan cheese
½ teaspoon garlic powder
1 teaspoon dried parsley
½ teaspoon dried oregano
115g shredded mozzarella cheese

1. In a round baking dish, pour 60g pasta sauce on the bottom of the dish. Place ¼ of the ground beef on top of the sauce. 2. In a small bowl, mix the ricotta, parsley, Parmesan, garlic powder, and oregano. Place dollops of half the mixture on top of the beef. 3. Sprinkle with ⅓ of the mozzarella. Repeat layers until all beef, ricotta mixture, sauce, and mozzarella are used, ending with the mozzarella on top. 4. Cover the dish with foil and place into the drawer. 5. Select BAKE, set the temperature to 185°C and set the time for 15 minutes. Select START/STOP to begin cooking. 6. In the last 2 minutes of cooking, remove the foil to brown the cheese. Serve immediately.

Marinated Steak Tips with Mushrooms

⏰ Prep Time: 10 minutes 🍳 Cook: 10 minutes 🍽 Serves: 4

680g sirloin, trimmed and cut into 1-inch pieces
230g brown mushrooms, halved
65g Worcestershire sauce
1 tablespoon Dijon mustard
1 tablespoon olive oil
1 teaspoon paprika
1 teaspoon crushed red pepper flakes
2 tablespoons chopped fresh parsley (optional)

1. Place the beef and mushrooms in a gallon-size resealable bag. In a small bowl, whisk together the Worcestershire, paprika, mustard, olive oil, and red pepper flakes. Pour the marinade into the bag and massage gently to ensure the beef and mushrooms are evenly coated. Seal the bag and refrigerate for at least 4 hours, preferably overnight. Remove from the refrigerator 30 minutes before cooking. 2. Drain and discard the marinade. Insert the crisper plate in the drawer in the lower position, place the steak and mushrooms in the drawer, and insert the drawer into the unit. 3. Select AIR FRY, set the temperature to 200°C and set the time to 10 minutes. Select START/STOP to begin cooking. Cook, pausing halfway through the cooking time to shake the drawer. 4. Transfer to a serving plate and top with the parsley, if desired.

Beef Meatballs and Spaghetti Zoodles

⏰ Prep Time: 15 minutes 🍳 Cook: 11-13 minutes 🍽 Serves: 6

455g ground beef
1½ teaspoons sea salt, plus more for seasoning
1 large egg, beaten
1 teaspoon gelatin
75g Parmesan cheese
2 teaspoons minced garlic
1 teaspoon Italian seasoning
Freshly ground black pepper
Avocado oil spray
Keto-friendly marinara sauce, such as Rao's Homemade®, for serving
170g courgette noodles, made using a spiraliser or store-bought

1. Place the ground beef in a large bowl and season with the salt. 2. Place the egg in a separate bowl and sprinkle with the gelatin. Allow to sit for 5 minutes. 3. Stir the gelatin mixture and pour it over the ground beef. Add the Parmesan, garlic, and Italian seasoning. Season with the salt and pepper. 4. Form the mixture into 1½-inch meatballs and place them on a plate. Cover with plastic wrap and refrigerate for at least 1 hour or overnight. 5. Spray the meatballs with the oil. Insert the crisper plate in the drawer in the lower position, place the meatballs in a single layer in the drawer, and insert the drawer into the unit. 6. Select AIR FRY, set the temperature to 200°C and set the time to 4 minutes. Select START/STOP to begin cooking. 7. Flip the meatballs and spray them with more oil. Cook for 4 minutes more, until an instant-read thermometer reads 70°C. Transfer the meatballs to a plate and allow them to rest. 8. While the meatballs are resting, heat the marinara in a saucepan on the stove over medium heat. 9. Place the courgette noodles in the drawer and cook at 200°C for 3 to 5 minutes. 10. To serve, place the courgette noodles in serving bowls. Top with the meatballs and warm marinara.

Air-Fried Rib Eye Steaks with Horseradish Cream

⏰ **Prep Time: 5 minutes**   🍳 **Cook: 10 minutes**   🍽 **Serves: 8**

910g rib eye steaks
Sea salt
Freshly ground black pepper
Unsalted butter, for serving
115g sour cream
75g heavy (whipping) cream
4 tablespoons prepared horseradish
1 teaspoon Dijon mustard
1 teaspoon apple cider vinegar
¼ teaspoon Swerve Confectioners sweetener

1. Pat the steaks dry. Season with the salt and pepper and let sit at room temperature for about 45 minutes. 2. Insert the crisper plate in the drawer in the lower position. Working in batches, place the steaks in a single layer in the drawer and insert the drawer into the unit. 3. Select AIR FRY, set the temperature to 200°C and set the time to 5 minutes. Select START/STOP to begin cooking. 4. Flip the steaks and cook for 5 minutes more, until an instant-read thermometer reads 50°C (or to your desired doneness). 5. Transfer the steaks to a plate and top each with a pat of butter. Tent with foil and let rest for 10 minutes. 6. Combine the sour cream, heavy cream, horseradish, Dijon mustard, vinegar, and Swerve in a bowl. Stir until smooth. 7. Serve the steaks with the horseradish cream.

Guacamole Bacon Burgers

⏰ **Prep Time: 15 minutes**   🍳 **Cook: 9 minutes**   🍽 **Serves: 8**

910g ground beef
2 teaspoons Taco Seasoning
Sea salt
Freshly ground black pepper
Avocado oil spray
2 large ripe avocados, peeled and pits removed
1 tablespoon freshly squeezed lime juice
½ teaspoon ground cumin
230g sliced bacon, cooked and crumbled
35g chopped red onion
1 tablespoon minced garlic
1 canned chipotle chilli in adobo sauce, seeded and chopped with sauce removed
1 small tomato, seeded and diced
5g fresh cilantro, chopped
Lettuce leaves or keto-friendly buns, for serving

1. In a large bowl, combine the ground beef and taco seasoning. Season with the salt and pepper. Mix with your hands until well-combined. Form the mixture into 8 patties, making them thinner in the centre for even cooking. Spray the patties with the oil. 2. Insert the crisper plate in the drawer in the lower position. Working in batches if necessary, place the patties in the drawer and insert the drawer into the unit. 3. Select ROAST, set the temperature to 175°C and set the time for 5 minutes. Select START/STOP to begin cooking. 4. Flip and cook for 4 minutes more, until the patties are cooked through and an instant-read thermometer reads 70°C. Let the burgers rest for 5 minutes before serving. 5. Meanwhile, mash the avocados in a medium bowl. Add the lime juice and cumin. Season with the salt and pepper. Stir to combine. Gently stir in the bacon, chipotle chilli, onion, garlic, tomato, and cilantro. Cover with plastic wrap, gently pressing it directly on the surface of the guacamole. Refrigerate until ready to serve. 6. Top each burger with a dollop of guacamole and serve in lettuce wraps or on keto-friendly buns.

Chinese-Style Spareribs

⏱ **Prep Time: 10 minutes** 🍲 **Cook: 30-35 minutes** ❖ **Serves: 4**

1 tablespoon sesame oil
1 tablespoon fermented black bean paste
1 tablespoon seasoned rice vinegar
1 tablespoon reduced-sodium soy sauce
1 tablespoon Swerve sugar replacement
1 teaspoon minced garlic
1 teaspoon grated fresh ginger
910g pork spareribs, cut into small pieces

1. In a small bowl, combine the sesame oil, black bean paste, soy sauce, Swerve, garlic, rice vinegar, and ginger. Stir until thoroughly combined. Transfer the marinade to a gallon-size resealable bag and add the ribs. Seal the bag and massage the ribs to coat with the marinade. Refrigerate for at least 4 hours, preferably overnight. 2. Insert the crisper plate in the drawer in the lower position. Working in batches if necessary, arrange the ribs in a single layer in the drawer and insert the drawer into the unit. 3. Select AIR FRY, set the temperature to 195°C and set the time to 30 minutes. Select START/STOP to begin cooking. Air fry for 30 to 35 minutes, until tender and browned, pausing halfway through the cooking time to turn the ribs. 4. When done, serve and enjoy.

Blue Cheese and Steak Salad with Balsamic Vinaigrette

⏱ **Prep Time: 15 minutes** 🍲 **Cook: 22 minutes** ❖ **Serves: 4**

2 tablespoons balsamic vinegar
2 tablespoons red wine vinegar
1 tablespoon Dijon mustard
1 tablespoon Swerve Confectioners or keto-friendly sweetener of choice
1 teaspoon minced garlic
Sea salt
Freshly ground black pepper
180ml extra-virgin olive oil
455g boneless sirloin steak
Avocado oil spray
1 small red onion, cut into ¼-inch-thick rounds
170g baby spinach
75g cherry tomatoes, halved
85g blue cheese, crumbled

1. In a blender, combine the balsamic vinegar, red wine vinegar, Swerve, Dijon mustard, and garlic. Season with the salt and pepper and process until smooth. With the blender running, drizzle in the olive oil. Process until well combined. Transfer to a jar with a tight-fitting lid and refrigerate until ready to serve (it will keep for up to 2 weeks). 2. Season the steak with the salt and pepper and let sit at room temperature for at least 45 minutes, time permitting. 3. Insert the crisper plate in the drawer in the lower position. Spray the steak with the oil and place it in the drawer. Insert the drawer into the unit. 4. Select AIR FRY, set the temperature to 200°C and set the time to 6 minutes. Select START/STOP to begin cooking. 5. Flip the steak and spray it with more oil. Cook for 6 minutes more for medium-rare or until the steak is done to your liking. 6. Transfer the steak to a plate, tent with a piece of aluminium foil, and allow it to rest. 7. Spray the onion slices with the oil and place them in the drawer. Cook at 200°C for 5 minutes. Flip the onion slices and spray them with more oil. Cook for 5 minutes more. 8. Slice the steak diagonally into thin strips. Place the spinach, onion slices, cherry tomatoes, and steak in a large bowl. Toss with the desired amount of dressing. Sprinkle with crumbled blue cheese and serve.

Chapter 6 Beef and Pork

Glazed Ham Steaks with Sweet Potatoes

⏰ Prep Time: 20 minutes 🍲 Cook: 15-17 minutes 🍽 Serves: 4

240ml freshly squeezed orange juice
110g packed light brown sugar
1 tablespoon Dijon mustard
½ teaspoon salt
½ teaspoon freshly ground black pepper
3 sweet potatoes, cut into small wedges
2 ham steaks (230g each), halved
1 to 2 tablespoons oil

1. In a large bowl, whisk the orange juice, brown sugar, Dijon, salt, and pepper until blended. Toss the sweet potato wedges with the brown sugar mixture. 2. Insert the crisper plate in the drawer in the lower position. Line the crisper plate with parchment paper and spritz with oil. 3. Place the sweet potato wedges on the parchment. 4. Insert the drawer into the unit. Select AIR FRY, set the temperature to 200°C and set the time to 10 minutes. Select START/STOP to begin cooking. 5. Place ham steaks on top of the sweet potatoes and brush everything with more of the orange juice mixture. 6. Cook for 3 minutes. Flip the ham and cook or 2 to 4 minutes more until the sweet potatoes are soft and the glaze has thickened. Cut the ham steaks in half to serve.

Spicy Baby Back Ribs

⏰ Prep Time: 5 minutes 🍲 Cook: 35 minutes 🍽 Serves: 2

2 teaspoons fine sea salt
1 teaspoon ground black pepper
2 teaspoons smoked paprika
1 teaspoon garlic powder
1 teaspoon onion powder
½ teaspoon chilli powder (optional, for a spicy kick)
1 rack baby back ribs, cut in half crosswise

1. Insert the crisper plate in the drawer in the lower position and spray the crisper plate with the avocado oil. 2. In a small bowl, combine the salt, pepper, and seasonings. Season the ribs on all sides with the seasoning mixture. 3. Place the ribs in the drawer and insert the drawer into the unit. Select AIR FRY, set the temperature to 175°C and set the time to 15 minutes. Select START/STOP to begin cooking. 4. Then flip the ribs over and cook for another 15 to 20 minutes, until the ribs are cooked through and the internal temperature reaches 60°C. 5. Store leftovers in an airtight container in the refrigerator for up to 4 days. Reheat in a preheated 175°C air fryer for 5 minutes, or until heated through.

| Chapter 6 Beef and Pork

Chapter 7 Desserts

- 62 Mini Peanut Butter Tarts
- 62 Chocolate and Peanut Butter Tart
- 63 Chocolate Lava Cake with Raspberry Sauce
- 63 Air Fryer Mixed Berry Pavlova
- 64 Fluffy Gingerbread Cake
- 64 Fresh Berry Cream Puffs
- 65 Baked Coconut Pie
- 65 Air Fried Cinnamon Doughnut Bites
- 66 Maple Pecan Squares
- 66 Chocolate Chip Pecan Biscotti
- 67 Tasty Chocolate Soufflés
- 67 Keto Almond Flour Cinnamon Rolls
- 68 Mini Chocolate Nut Pies
- 68 Bread Pudding with Cranberries and Raisins

Mini Peanut Butter Tarts

⏰ Prep Time: 25 minutes   🍳 Cook: 12-15 minutes   🍽 Serves: 8

120g pecans
110g finely ground blanched almond flour
2 tablespoons unsalted butter, at room temperature
70g plus 2 tablespoons Swerve Confectioners sweetener, divided
120g heavy (whipping) cream
2 tablespoons mascarpone cheese
115g cream cheese
125g sugar-free peanut butter
1 teaspoon pure vanilla extract
⅛ teaspoon sea salt
120g stevia-sweetened chocolate chips, such as Lily's Sweets brand
1 tablespoon coconut oil
30g chopped peanuts or pecans

1. Place the pecans in the bowl of a food processor; process until they are finely ground. 2. Transfer the ground pecans to a medium bowl and stir in the almond flour. Add the butter and 2 tablespoons of Swerve, and stir until the mixture becomes wet and crumbly. 3. Divide the mixture among 8 silicone muffin cups, pressing the crust firmly with your fingers into the bottom and part way up the sides of each cup. 4. Insert the crisper plate in the drawer in the lower position, place the muffin cups in the drawer, working in batches if necessary, and insert the drawer into the unit. 5. Select AIR FRY, set the temperature to 150°C and set the time to 12 minutes. Select START/STOP to begin cooking. Cook for 12 to 15 minutes, until the crusts begin to brown. Remove the cups from the air fryer and set them aside to cool. 6. In the bowl of a stand mixer, combine the heavy cream and mascarpone cheese. Beat until peaks form. Transfer to a large bowl. 7. In the same stand mixer bowl, combine the cream cheese, remaining 70g of Swerve, peanut butter, vanilla, and salt. Beat at medium-high speed until smooth. 8. Reduce the speed to low and add the heavy cream mixture back a spoonful at a time, beating after each addition. 9. Spoon the peanut butter mixture over the crusts, and freeze the tarts for 30 minutes. 10. Place the chocolate chips and coconut oil in the top of a double boiler over high heat. Stir until melted, then remove from the heat. 11. Drizzle the melted chocolate over the peanut butter tarts. Top with the chopped nuts and freeze the tarts for another 15 minutes, until set. 12. Store the peanut butter tarts in an airtight container in the refrigerator for up to 1 week or in the freezer for up to 1 month.

Chocolate and Peanut Butter Tart

⏰ Prep Time: 20 minutes   🍳 Cook: 10 minutes   🍽 Serves: 10

110g almond flour
30g Swerve sugar replacement
6 tablespoons coconut oil, melted, divided
1 teaspoon vanilla extract, divided
40g peanut flour
40g plus 1 tablespoon powdered Swerve sugar replacement, divided
195g smooth peanut butter
170g sugar-free chocolate chips

1. Line a round baking pan with parchment paper and set aside. 2. In a bowl, combine the almond flour and Swerve. Add 3 tablespoons of the melted coconut oil and ½ teaspoon of the vanilla. Stir, pressing with the back of a spoon or spatula, until a crumbly dough forms. Press the dough into the bottom of the prepared pan. 3. Place the pan in the drawer and insert the drawer into the unit. 4. Select BAKE, set the temperature to 175°C and set the time for 10 minutes. Select START/STOP to begin cooking. Bake for 10 minutes until the edges are golden. Let cool for a few minutes until the top is firm and the pan is cool enough to handle. 5. Meanwhile, in a medium bowl, mix together the peanut flour and 40g of the powdered Swerve. Add the peanut butter and the remaining ½ teaspoon vanilla. Mix well, pressing with the back of a spatula or spoon, until thoroughly combined. Spread the peanut butter mixture into the pan, using the back of a silicone spatula to ensure an even layer. 6. In a medium microwavable bowl, combine the chocolate chips and the remaining 3 tablespoons coconut oil. Heat on high in the microwave for 1 to 2 minutes, stirring every 20 seconds, until completely melted. Whisk in the remaining 1 tablespoon powdered Swerve. Pour the chocolate over the peanut butter layer and spread evenly. 7. Let the tart cool completely, until the chocolate is solid, before cutting into wedges.

Chocolate Lava Cake with Raspberry Sauce

⏱ **Prep Time: 15 minutes**   🍱 **Cook: 12 minutes**   🍽 **Serves: 4**

80g semisweet chocolate chips
60g milk chocolate chips
55g butter
2 large eggs
1 large egg yolk
50g granulated sugar
3 tablespoons powdered sugar
1 teaspoon vanilla
4 tablespoons all-purpose flour
¼ teaspoon baking powder
Pinch sea salt
Unsalted butter, at room temperature
2 teaspoons cocoa powder
4 teaspoons raspberry jam
120g fresh raspberries
1 tablespoon freshly squeezed lemon juice

1. In a small microwave-safe bowl, melt the semisweet chocolate chips, butter, and milk chocolate chips in the microwave on medium power, 2 to 3 minutes. Remove and stir until combined and smooth, then set aside. 2. In a medium bowl, beat together the eggs and egg yolk. Gradually add the granulated and powdered sugars, beating until the mixture is fluffy and lighter yellow in colour. Beat in the vanilla. 3. Add the flour, baking powder, and salt and mix until combined. Fold in the chocolate and butter mixture. 4. Grease four 115g glass heatproof ramekins with the unsalted butter. Sprinkle ½ teaspoon cocoa power in each ramekin and shake to coat. Shake out the excess cocoa powder. 5. Fill the ramekins half full with the batter. Top each with a teaspoon of the raspberry jam. Cover the jam with the rest of the batter. 6. Insert the crisper plate in the drawer in the lower position, place the ramekins in the drawer, and insert the drawer into the unit. You may be able to bake all four at one time, or just two at a time. 7. Select BAKE, set the temperature to 190°C and set the time for 9 minutes. Select START/STOP to begin cooking. Bake for 9 to 12 minutes or until the edges of the cake are set; the centre will still be jiggly. 8. While the cakes are baking, place the raspberries and lemon juice in a small saucepan. Bring to a simmer over medium-low heat. Simmer for 2 to 4 minutes or until a sauce forms. Remove from heat and set aside. 9. Remove the ramekins and let cool on a wire rack for 5 minutes. Run a knife around the edge of each ramekin and invert each cake onto a serving plate. Top with the raspberry sauce and serve.

Air Fryer Mixed Berry Pavlova

⏱ **Prep Time: 10 minutes**   🍱 **Cook: 45 minutes**   🍽 **Serves: 4**

3 large egg whites
Pinch sea salt
135g granulated sugar
1 teaspoon cornstarch
1 teaspoon apple cider vinegar
120g heavy (whipping) cream
2 tablespoons powdered sugar
45g blueberries
40g raspberries
50g chopped strawberries
1 teaspoon honey

1. In a very clean mixing bowl, beat the egg whites and salt with a hand mixer. 2. When soft peaks start to form, beat in the granulated sugar, one tablespoon at a time. Keep beating until the meringue is glossy and forms stiff peaks when the beater is lifted. 3. Fold in the cornstarch and vinegar. 4. Cut a piece of parchment paper the same size as the bottom of a round pan. Put a dot of the meringue mixture on the bottom of the pan and add the parchment paper; this helps the paper stay in place. 5. Put the meringue mixture on the parchment paper, forming it into a disc and flattening the top and sides with a spatula. 6. Place the pan in the drawer and insert the drawer into the unit. Select BAKE, set the temperature to 150°C and set the time for 40 minutes. Select START/STOP to begin cooking. Bake for 40 to 45 minutes or until the meringue is dry to the touch. Turn off the air fryer, pull the drawer out about an inch, and let the meringue cool for 1 hour. 7. Remove the meringue from the drawer and cool completely on a wire rack. 8. In a small bowl, beat the cream with the powdered sugar until soft peaks form. 9. Turn the meringue over so the bottom is on top. Spread the cream over the meringue, then top with the blueberries, raspberries, and strawberries and drizzle with the honey. Serve immediately, or cover and refrigerate for up to 1 day.

Chapter 7 Desserts | 63

Fluffy Gingerbread Cake

⏱ **Prep Time: 15 minutes** 🍲 **Cook: 27 minutes** ❖ **Serves: 6**

120g all-purpose flour
1 teaspoon ground ginger
½ teaspoon cinnamon
½ teaspoon baking soda
¼ teaspoon sea salt
⅛ teaspoon nutmeg
⅛ teaspoon ground cardamom
65g brown sugar
115g honey
80ml milk
1 large egg yolk
Unsalted butter, at room temperature

1. In a medium bowl, combine the flour, ginger, baking soda, salt, cinnamon, nutmeg, and cardamom and mix well. 2. In another medium bowl, combine the brown sugar, milk, honey, and egg yolk and beat until combined. 3. Stir the honey mixture into the flour mixture just until combined. 4. Grease a round pan with the unsalted butter. Cut a piece of parchment paper to fit the pan and grease it. Pour in the batter. Cover the pan tightly with aluminium foil and poke a few holes in the foil with the tip of a knife. 5. Place the pan in the drawer and insert the drawer into the unit. 6. Select BAKE, set the temperature to 160°C and set the time for 22 minutes. Select START/STOP to begin cooking. Bake for 22 to 27 minutes or until a toothpick inserted near the centre of the gingerbread comes out with only a few moist crumbs. 7. Remove the pan from the drawer and cool on a wire rack for 20 minutes. Cut into wedges and serve.

Fresh Berry Cream Puffs

⏱ **Prep Time: 15 minutes** 🍲 **Cook: 24 minutes** ❖ **Serves: 6**

60g raspberries
35g chopped strawberries
35g blueberries
1 tablespoon honey
6 tablespoons water
55g butter
120g all-purpose flour
Pinch sea salt
2 large eggs

1. Combine the raspberries, strawberries, and blueberries with the honey in a small bowl and mix gently; set aside. 2. Combine the water and butter in a medium saucepan over high heat and bring to a rolling boil. Reduce the heat to medium and add the flour and salt. Beat well until the dough forms a ball and pulls away from the sides of the pan. 3. Remove the pan from the heat. Using an electric hand mixer, beat in the eggs, one at a time, until the dough is smooth and shiny. 4. Line a round cookie sheet with parchment paper. Working in batches, spoon three rounded tablespoons of the dough onto the cookie sheet (half the dough), 1 inch apart. 5. Place the sheet in the drawer and insert the drawer into the unit. 6. Select BAKE, set the temperature to 200°C and set the time for 18 minutes. Select START/STOP to begin cooking. Bake for 18 to 24 minutes or until the cream puffs are puffed and golden brown. Remove the cream puffs and let cool on a wire rack. Repeat with remaining dough. 7. Slice the cream puffs in half crosswise. Remove any loose strands of dough and fill with the fruit.

| Chapter 7 Desserts

Baked Coconut Pie

⏰ Prep Time: 20 minutes 🍱 Cook: 45-50 minutes 🍽 Serves: 6

55g plus 15g unsweetened shredded coconut, divided
2 eggs
360ml milk
60g granulated Swerve sugar replacement
40g coconut flour
55g unsalted butter, melted
1½ teaspoons vanilla extract
¼ teaspoon salt
2 tablespoons powdered Swerve sugar replacement (optional)
45g sugar-free whipped topping (optional)

1. Spread 15g of the coconut in the bottom of a pie plate. Place the plate in the drawer and insert the drawer into the unit. 2. Select BAKE, set the temperature to 175°C and set the time for 5 minutes. Select START/STOP to begin cooking. Cook until golden brown. Transfer the coconut to a small bowl and set aside for garnish. Brush the pie plate with the vegetable oil and set aside. 3. In a large bowl, combine the remaining 55g shredded coconut, eggs, milk, coconut flour, butter, vanilla, granulated Swerve, and salt. Whisk until smooth. Pour the batter into the prepared pie plate and bake for 40 to 45 minutes, or until a toothpick inserted into the centre of the pie comes out clean. Check halfway through the baking time and rotate the pan, if necessary, for even baking. 4. Remove the pie from the air fryer and let cool completely on a baking rack. Garnish with the reserved toasted coconut and the powdered Swerve or sugar-free whipped topping, if desired. Cover and refrigerate leftover pie for up to 3 days.

Air Fried Cinnamon Doughnut Bites

⏰ Prep Time: 20 minutes 🍱 Cook: 6 minutes 🍽 Serves: 5

180ml water
8 tablespoons unsalted butter, divided
4 tablespoons Swerve sugar replacement, divided
½ teaspoon salt
80g almond flour
55g coconut flour
1 teaspoon baking powder
Zest of 1 orange
2 eggs
1 teaspoon vanilla extract
2 teaspoons ground cinnamon

1. Line a small baking sheet with parchment paper and set aside. 2. In a medium pot over medium-high heat, combine the water, 5 tablespoons of the butter, 2 tablespoons of the Swerve, and the salt. Bring the mixture to boil, whisking until the butter is melted. Remove from the heat and let cool for a few minutes. 3. In a large mixing bowl, whisk together the almond flour, coconut flour, baking powder, and orange zest. Add the dry ingredients to the water mixture in the pot. Stir briskly. The mixture should be the consistency of loose mashed potatoes. 4. In a small bowl, whisk the eggs and vanilla. Add the egg mixture to the pot and whisk until smooth. Let sit for 10 to 15 minutes until the dough thickens. 5. Transfer the dough to a resealable bag. Cut a ¼-inch tip from one corner of the bag. Squeeze about 20 1½-inch mounds onto parchment paper. Freeze for 45 minutes or until hard. 6. Insert the crisper plate in the drawer in the lower position. Working in batches if necessary, place the doughnuts in the drawer and insert the drawer into the unit. 7. Select AIR FRY, set the temperature to 200°C and set the time to 6 minutes. Select START/STOP to begin cooking. Air Fry until brown and crisp. 8. In a small shallow bowl, combine the cinnamon and the remaining 2 tablespoons Swerve. In another small, shallow microwavable bowl, melt the remaining 3 tablespoons butter in the microwave on high for 30 seconds to 1 minute. While the doughnuts are warm, brush with the melted butter and roll in the cinnamon-Swerve mixture. Serve warm.

Chapter 7 Desserts

Maple Pecan Squares

⏱ **Prep Time: 20 minutes** 🎁 **Cook: 22 minutes** ❦ **Serves: 8**

110g finely ground blanched almond flour
1½ tablespoons Swerve Confectioners sweetener
5 tablespoons cold unsalted butter, cut into cubes
3 teaspoons pure vanilla extract, divided
55g (4 tablespoons) unsalted butter, at room temperature
60g brown sugar substitute, such as Sukrin Gold
60g maple syrup substitute, such as ChocZero sugar-free maple syrup
1 tablespoon heavy (whipping) cream
150g chopped pecans or other keto-friendly nuts

1. Line a pan that is at least 2 inches deep with parchment paper. If you have it, a small springform pan works beautifully here. Otherwise, use enough parchment paper so that you have some overhang to help you lift the pastry from the pan once it has cooled. 2. Stir together the almond flour and Swerve in the bowl of a stand mixer. Add the cold butter and 1 teaspoon of vanilla and beat until the mixture comes together, 3 to 4 minutes. 3. Press the crust into the prepared pan. Place the pan in the drawer and insert the drawer into the unit. 4. Select BAKE, set the temperature to 160°C and set the time for 8 minutes. Select START/STOP to begin cooking. 5. Remove the drawer from the air fryer and allow the crust to cool. 6. While the crust cooks, combine the 55g of butter, brown sugar substitute, and maple syrup substitute in a saucepan over medium heat. Cook until the butter is melted and the mixture is thick and bubbly, about 5 minutes. Stir in the heavy cream, remaining 2 teaspoons of vanilla, and chopped pecans. 7. Pour the mixture on top of the crust. Place the drawer back in the air fryer and cook for 14 minutes or until set. 8. Remove the pan from the air fryer and let cool completely. Carefully remove the pastry from the pan and cut it into squares.

Chocolate Chip Pecan Biscotti

⏱ **Prep Time: 15 minutes** 🎁 **Cook: 20-22 minutes** ❦ **Serves: 10**

135g finely ground blanched almond flour
¾ teaspoon baking powder
½ teaspoon xanthan gum
¼ teaspoon sea salt
3 tablespoons unsalted butter, at room temperature
40g Swerve Confectioners sweetener
1 large egg, beaten
1 teaspoon pure vanilla extract
40g chopped pecans
60g stevia-sweetened chocolate chips, such as Lily's Sweets brand
Melted stevia-sweetened chocolate chips and chopped pecans, for topping (optional)

1. In a large bowl, combine the almond flour, xanthan gum, baking powder, and salt. 2. Line a cake pan that fits inside your air fryer with parchment paper. 3. In the bowl of a stand mixer, beat together the butter and Swerve. Add the beaten egg and vanilla, and beat for about 3 minutes. 4. Add the almond flour mixture to the butter-and-egg mixture and beat until just combined. 5. Stir in the chocolate chips and pecans. 6. Transfer the dough to the prepared pan and press it into the bottom. 7. Place the pan in the drawer and insert the drawer into the unit. 8. Select BAKE, set the temperature to 160°C and set the time for 12 minutes. Select START/STOP to begin cooking. 9. Remove the cake pan from the air fryer and let cool for 15 minutes. Cut the cookie into thin strips with a sharp knife, then return the strips to the cake pan with the bottom sides facing up. Cook at 150°C for 8 to 10 minutes. 10. Remove the cake pan from the air fryer and let cool completely on a wire rack. If desired, dip one side of each biscotti piece into the melted chocolate chips and top with the chopped pecans. Serve and enjoy.

Chapter 7 Desserts

Tasty Chocolate Soufflés

⏱ **Prep Time: 10 minutes** 🍳 **Cook: 14 minutes** 🍽 **Serves: 2**

Butter and sugar for greasing the ramekins
85g semi-sweet chocolate, chopped
55g unsalted butter
2 eggs, yolks and white separated
3 tablespoons sugar
½ teaspoon pure vanilla extract
2 tablespoons all-purpose flour
Powdered sugar, for dusting the finished soufflés
Heavy cream, for serving

1. Butter and sugar two 170g ramekins. (Butter the ramekins and then coat the butter with sugar by shaking it around in the ramekin and dumping out any excess.) 2. Melt the chocolate and butter in the microwave or double boiler. In a separate bowl, beat the egg yolks vigorously. Add the sugar and the vanilla extract and beat well again. Drizzle in the chocolate and butter, mixing well. Stir in the flour and mix until there are no lumps. 3. In a separate bowl, whip the egg whites to soft peak stage (the point at which the whites can almost stand up on the end of your whisk). Gently pour the whipped egg whites into the chocolate mixture gently and in stages. 4. Carefully pour the batter into the buttered ramekins, leaving about ½-inch at the top. (depending on how fluffy the batter is, you may have some extra batter, so you may be able to squeeze out a third soufflé if you want.) Place the ramekins into the drawer and insert the drawer into the unit. Select BAKE, set the temperature to 165°C and set the time for 14 minutes. Select START/STOP to begin cooking. The soufflés should have risen nicely and be brown on top. (Don't worry if the top gets a little dark – you'll be covering it with powdered sugar in the next step.) 5. Dust with the powdered sugar and serve immediately with the heavy cream to pour over the top at the table.

Keto Almond Flour Cinnamon Rolls

⏱ **Prep Time: 20 minutes** 🍳 **Cook: 16-18 minutes** 🍽 **Serves: 8**

3 tablespoons unsalted butter, at room temperature
90g brown sugar substitute, such as Sukrin Gold
1 teaspoon ground cinnamon
165g finely ground blanched almond flour
¼ teaspoon sea salt
¼ teaspoon baking soda
¼ teaspoon xanthan gum
1 large egg, at room temperature
2 tablespoons unsalted butter, melted and cooled
1 tablespoon Swerve Confectioners sweetener
Avocado oil spray
Almond Glaze, for serving

1. In the bowl of a stand mixer, beat together the butter, brown sugar substitute, and cinnamon. Set aside. 2. In a large bowl, combine the almond flour, salt, baking soda, and xanthan gum. 3. In a separate bowl, beat the egg. Stir in the cooled melted butter and Swerve until combined. 4. Add the egg-and-butter mixture to the flour mixture and knead with clean hands until the dough is smooth. 5. Spray a large bowl with oil, add the dough, and turn to coat in the oil. Cover and refrigerate for 30 minutes. 6. Place the dough on a piece of parchment paper and form it into a rectangle. Put another piece of parchment on top of the dough and roll out the dough to a large rectangle, about ¼-inch thick. 7. Spread the butter and brown sugar mixture on top of the dough, and then roll up the dough from the long side. (Use the parchment paper to help if needed.) 8. Slice the rolled dough into 8 equal-size pieces, and arrange these in a parchment paper–lined cake pan that fits inside your air fryer. 9. Place the pan in the drawer and insert the drawer into the unit. Select BAKE, set the temperature to 150°C and set the time for 16 minutes. Select START/STOP to begin cooking. Cook for 16 to 18 minutes, until the tops of the rolls are lightly browned. 10. Let the rolls cool for 5 minutes, then invert them onto a plate. Sprinkle any cinnamon sugar mixture that has collected on the bottom of the pan over the top of the rolls. 11. Drizzle the almond glaze over the cinnamon rolls and serve warm.

Mini Chocolate Nut Pies

⏲ **Prep Time:: 15 minutes**   🍲 **Cook: 25 minutes**   🍽 **Serves: 10**

150g pecans
½ teaspoon sea salt
1 egg white
150g macadamia nuts, pecans, or a combination
80g plus 2 tablespoons stevia-sweetened chocolate chips, such as Lily's Sweets brand, divided
10g brown sugar substitute, such as Sukrin Gold
3 tablespoons maple syrup alternative, such as ChocZero sugar-free maple syrup
2 tablespoons unsalted butter
2 tablespoons heavy (whipping) cream
1 teaspoon vanilla extract
2 large eggs, beaten

1. Place the pecans and salt in the bowl of a food processor. Process until the nuts are very finely chopped. Transfer to a small bowl. 2. Place the egg white in the bowl of an electric mixer, and mix at high speed until stiff peaks form. Stir the egg white into the chopped pecans. Press the mixture into the bottom of 10 silicone muffin cups. 3. Insert the crisper plate in the drawer in the lower position, place the muffin cups in the drawer in a single layer, working in batches if necessary, and insert the drawer into the unit. Select AIR FRY, set the temperature to 150°C and set the time to 7 minutes. Select START/STOP to begin cooking. 4. Remove the drawer from the air fryer. Allow the muffin cups to cool slightly before removing them from the drawer. 5. While the crusts are cooling, pulse the macadamia nuts in the food processor until coarsely chopped. Transfer to a medium bowl and toss with 2 tablespoons of chocolate chips. Divide the mixture among the muffin cups. 6. Place the brown sugar substitute, maple syrup, and butter in a small saucepan over medium-high heat. Cook until the butter is melted and the sugars are dissolved. Stir in the cream and vanilla. Remove the pan from the heat and allow the mixture to cool slightly, then stir in the beaten eggs. 7. Pour the mixture over the nuts in the silicone cups, and return the cups to the drawer. Set the air fryer to 150°C and cook for 12 minutes. Remove the drawer from the air fryer. Once the pies are cool enough to handle, remove them from the drawer. 8. Place the remaining 80g of chocolate chips in a glass bowl, and heat them in the microwave for about 1 minute, until melted. Stir well. (You can also melt the chocolate in the top of a double boiler.) Drizzle the chocolate over the pies and allow it to set before serving.

Bread Pudding with Cranberries and Raisins

⏲ **Prep Time: 20 minutes**   🍲 **Cook: 35 minutes**   🍽 **Serves: 4**

177g heavy (whipping) cream
120ml whole milk
45g brown sugar
2 large egg yolks
3 tablespoons butter, melted
2 tablespoons honey
1 teaspoon vanilla
Pinch sea salt
440g bread cubes
30g dried cranberries
35g golden raisins
Unsalted butter, at room temperature

1. In a large bowl, combine the cream, milk, brown sugar, butter, honey, vanilla, egg yolks, and salt and mix well. 2. Stir in the bread cubes. Stir in the cranberries and raisins. Let stand for 15 minutes. 3. Grease the bottom and sides of a springform pan with the unsalted butter. Add the bread mixture. 4. Place the pan in the drawer and insert the drawer into the unit. 5. Select BAKE, set the temperature to 175°C and set the time for 30 minutes. Select START/STOP to begin cooking. Bake for 30 to 35 minutes or until the bread pudding is set and golden brown on top. 6. Remove from the drawer and cool for 20 minutes, then serve.

| Chapter 7 Desserts

Conclusion

In conclusion, this complete Ninja Air Fryer Cookbook offers a comprehensive guide to exploring the endless possibilities of your Ninja Air Fryer. With its emphasis on quick, easy, and healthy meals, this book is perfect for anyone looking to simplify their cooking while still enjoying delicious, satisfying dishes. The recipes inside are designed to help you make the most of your air fryer's capabilities, from crispy snacks to hearty meals and everything in between.

By combining convenience with creativity, this cookbook allows you to enjoy the flavours of fried foods without the guilt, making it ideal for those who want to eat healthier without compromising on taste. The colourful images throughout the book will keep you inspired, and the practical advice will help you achieve professional results in your own kitchen.

If you're ready to elevate your cooking game and make the most of your Ninja Air Fryer Max, this cookbook is the perfect tool. Whether you're a beginner or an experienced cook, the variety and versatility of recipes will suit all tastes and dietary needs, helping you create meals that are both easy and enjoyable.

Appendix Recipes Index

A
Air Fried Barbecued Riblets 55
Air Fried Cheddar Sandwich 28
Air Fried Cinnamon Doughnut Bites 65
Air Fried Stuffed Mushrooms 33
Air Fried Vegan Chimichanga 24
Air Fryer Fried Green Tomatoes 23
Air Fryer Jerk Chicken Thighs 35
Air Fryer Mixed Berry Pavlova 63
Air-Fried Cheese Sandwich 26
Air-Fried Rib Eye Steaks with Horseradish Cream 58
Authentic Chicken Parmesan 35

B
Bacon Wrapped Jalapeño Poppers 30
Baked Coconut Pie 65
Baked Sweet Potatoes with Honey Butter 23
Banana Walnut Breakfast Muffins 16
Beef Lasagna Casserole 56
Beef Meatballs and Spaghetti Zoodles 57
Blackened Shrimp Tacos with Coleslaw 50
Blue Cheese and Steak Salad with Balsamic Vinaigrette 59
Brazilian Tempero Baiano Chicken Drumsticks 37
Bread Pudding with Cranberries and Raisins 68
Brown Sugar Streusel Donuts 17

C
Cheesy Breakfast Sandwich 14
Cheesy German Apple Pancakes 18
Cheesy Refried Bean Taquitos 24
Cheesy Rice Stuffed Peppers 22
Chinese Ginger-Scallion Fish 46
Chinese Vegetable Fried Rice 22
Chinese-Style Spareribs 59
Chocolate and Peanut Butter Tart 62
Chocolate Chip Pecan Biscotti 66
Chocolate Lava Cake with Raspberry Sauce 63
Cinnamon Spiced Nuts 32
Classic Nashville Hot Chicken 40
Country-Style Barbecue Ribs 53
Cranberry Oatmeal Muffins 17
Cranberry Orange Muffin 15
Crispy Breaded Pork Chops 56
Crispy Buffalo Cauliflower 21
Crispy Buttermilk Catfish Strips 48
Crispy Chinese Five-Spice Pork Belly 54
Crispy Coconut Shrimp 44
Crispy Fish Sticks with Tartar Sauce 46
Crispy French Toast with Pecans 15
Crispy Jalapeño Poppers 29
Crispy Kale Chips 30
Crispy Pickle-Brined Fried Chicken 36
Crispy Potato Chips 28
Crispy Sweet Potato Chips 30

D
Delicious Bang Bang Shrimp 47
Delicious Tandoori Chicken Thighs 36

E
Easy Apple Fritters 16
Easy Sweet Potato Fries 21
Easy Tuna Patty Sliders 49
Feta and Spinach Stuffed Chicken Breasts 37
Fluffy Gingerbread Cake 64

F
Fresh Berry Cream Puffs 64

G
Garlic Butter Chicken 42
Garlic Chicken Wings with Green Beans and Rice 39
Glazed Ham Steaks with Sweet Potatoes 60
Greek Street Taco Hand Pies 33
Greek Turkey Burgers with Tzatziki Sauce 38
Guacamole Bacon Burgers 58

H
Hearty Crab Stuffed Salmon Roast 50
Homemade Crispy Fish and Chips 48
Homemade Mozzarella Cheese Sticks 28
Homestyle Fish Sticks 49
Honey Lemon Roasted Pork Loin 53
Honey Roasted Baby Carrots 21

I
Italian Frittata with Tomato and Cheese 19

J
Jalapeño Cheese Balls 32

K
Keto Almond Flour Cinnamon Rolls 67

L
Lime Shrimp with Garlic Peanuts 47
Loaded Baked Potato Skins 29
Low-Carb Tuna Patties with Spicy Sriracha Sauce 45

M
Maple Bacon Wrapped Chicken Breasts 40
Maple Pecan Squares 66
Marinated Ginger Chicken 42
Marinated Steak Tips with Mushrooms 57
Mini Chocolate Nut Pies 68
Mini Peanut Butter Tarts 62
Mixed Vegetable Hash 19

N
Nutritious Cucumber and Salmon Salad 44

P
Parmesan Courgette Chips with Lemon Aioli 31
Parmesan Dill Fried Pickles 31
Peppercorn-Crusted Beef Tenderloin 55

R
Roasted Chilean Sea Bass with Olive Relish 51
Roasted Rosemary Red Potatoes 22

S
Savoury Baked Tofu 13
Scrambled Eggs with Mushrooms 18
Sesame Crusted Tofu Steaks 25
Sesame-Crusted Salmon 45
Spicy Baby Back Ribs 60
Spicy Black Bean Turkey Burgers with Avocado Spread 39
Spicy Orange Shrimp 51
Spicy Pork Tenderloin with Avocado Lime Sauce 54
Spinach and Feta Chicken Meatballs 38

T
Tamale Pie with Cornmeal Crust 26
Tasty Chocolate Soufflés 67
Teriyaki Chicken Drumsticks 41
Thai Courgette Turkey Meatballs 41
Tofu Breakfast Sandwiches 14
Tomato and Spinach Stuffed Portobello Mushrooms 25

V
Vegetable Breakfast Tacos 13

Printed in Great Britain
by Amazon